# LOST RIVERS MOSAIC PAINTINGS

1400 hand-painted Emaux de Briare mosaic tiles, 2.5 x 2.5 cm.
Graphite, Porcelaine 150 paint and gold leaf

Nick Rands  2018

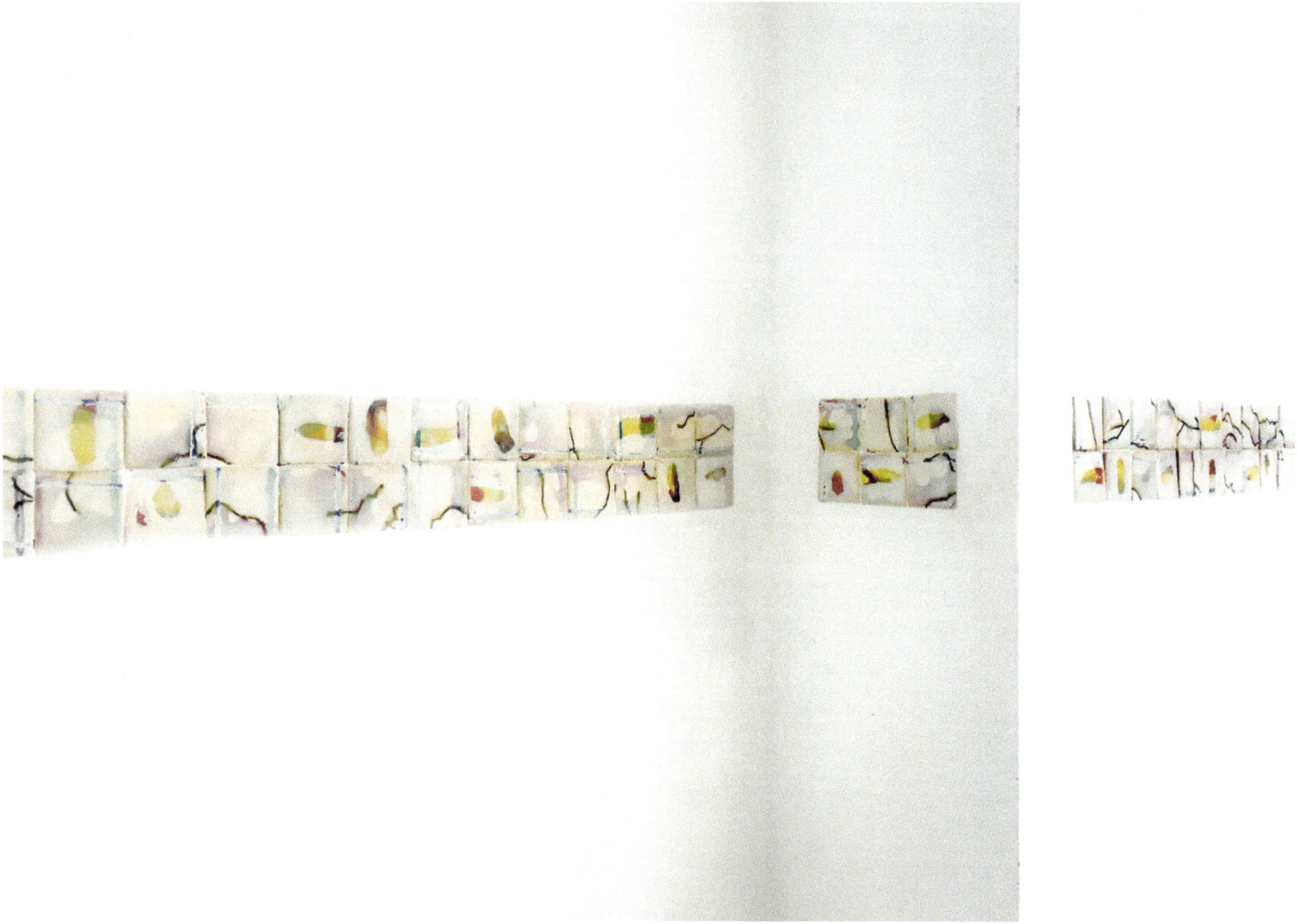

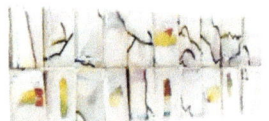

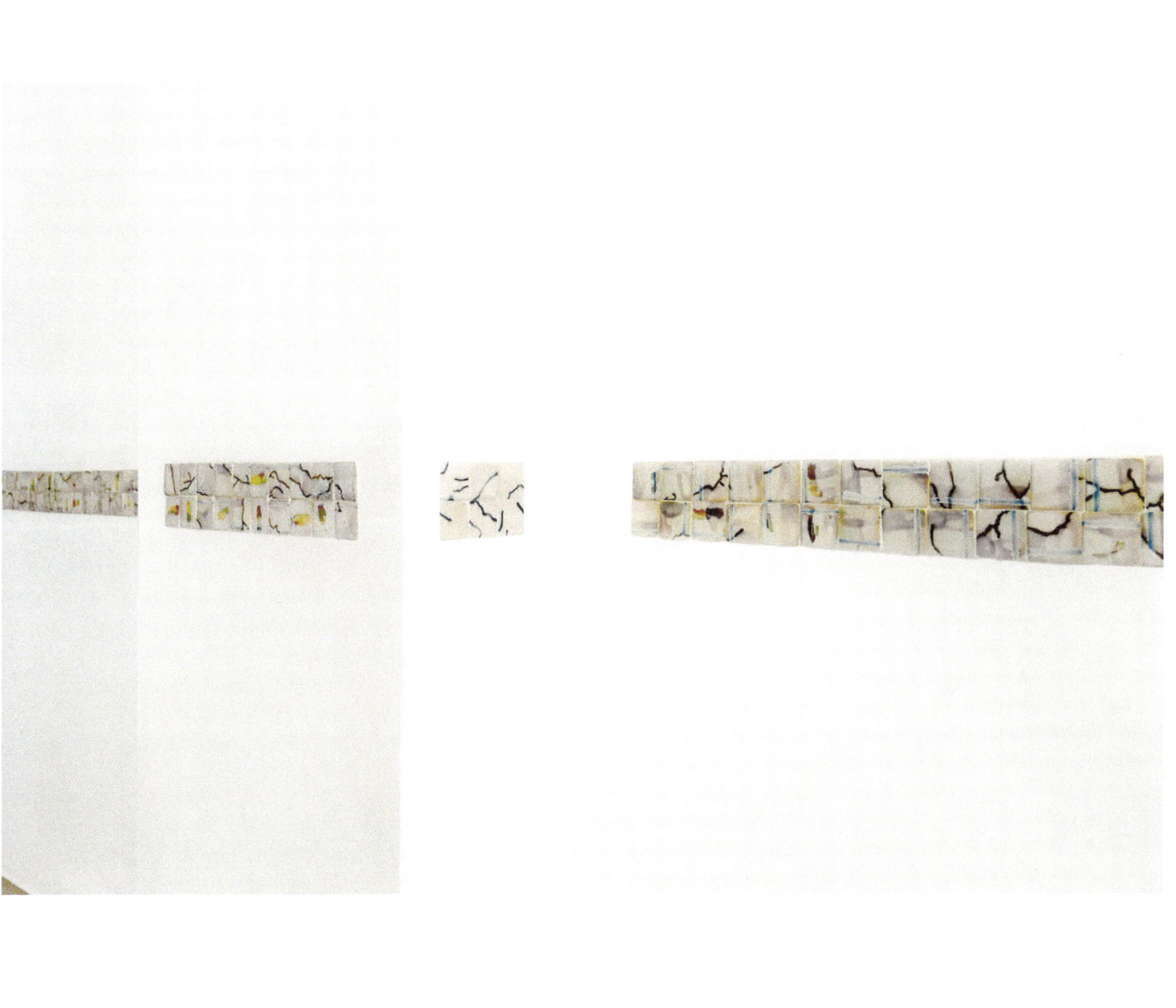

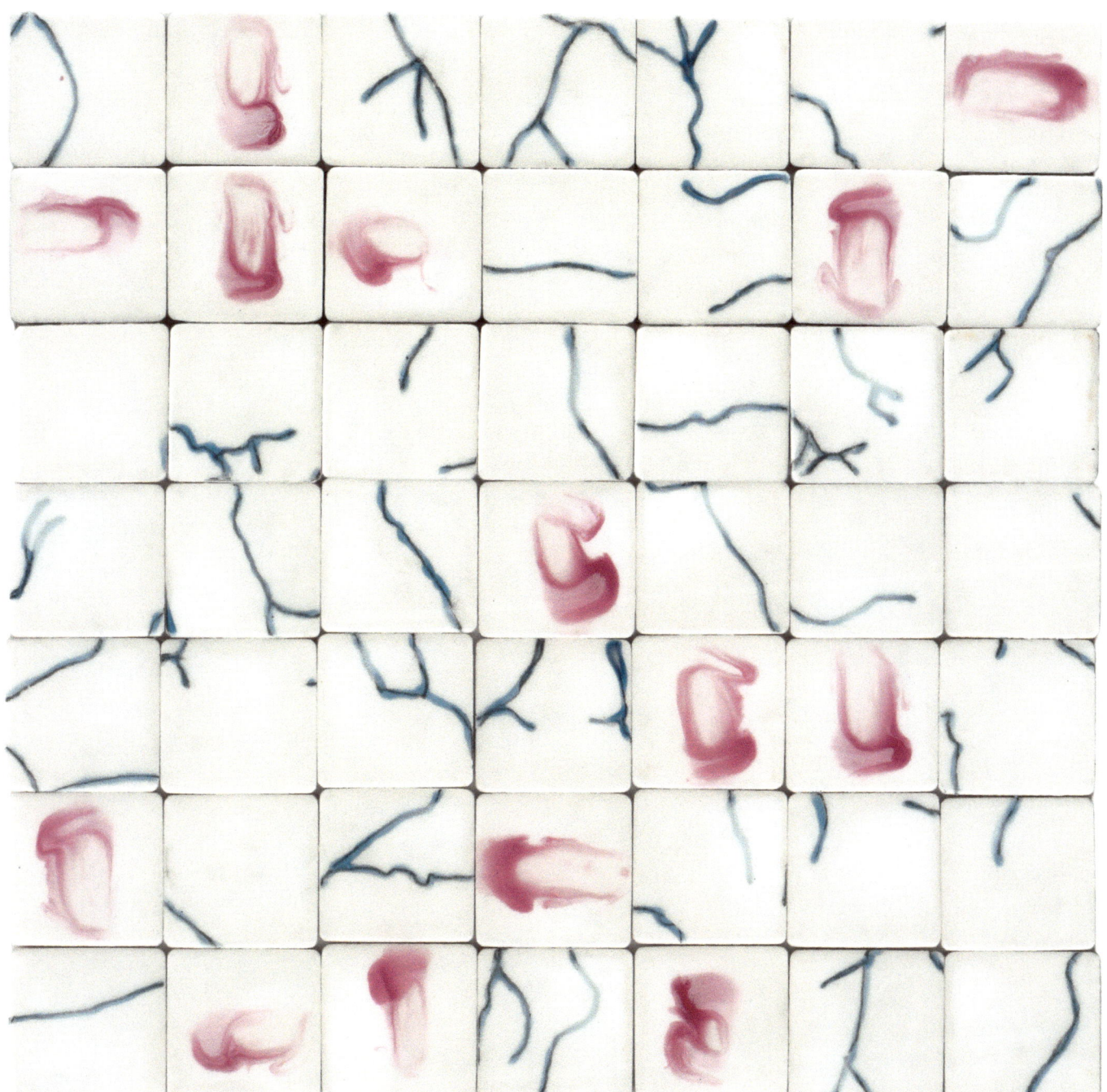

1

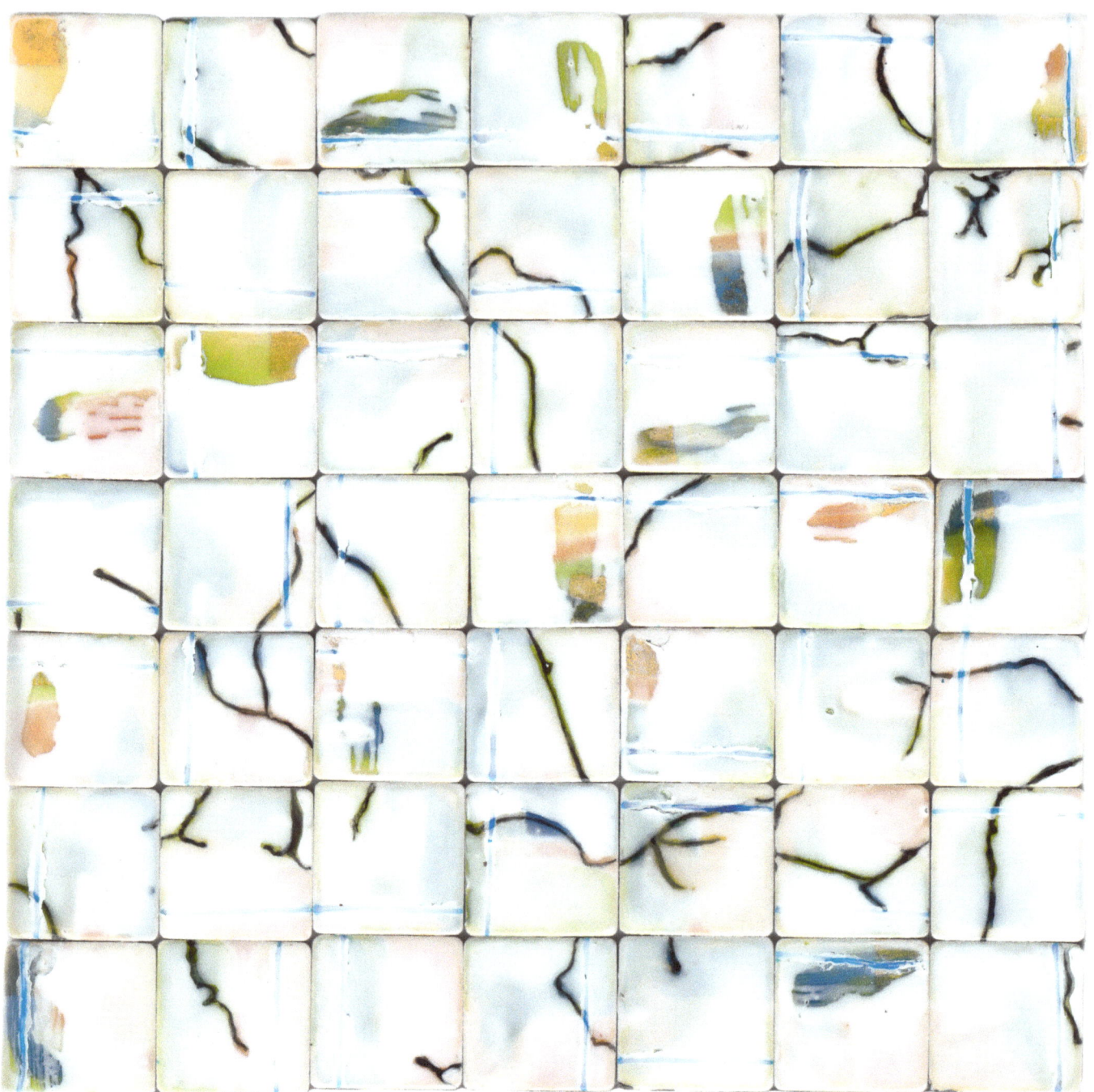

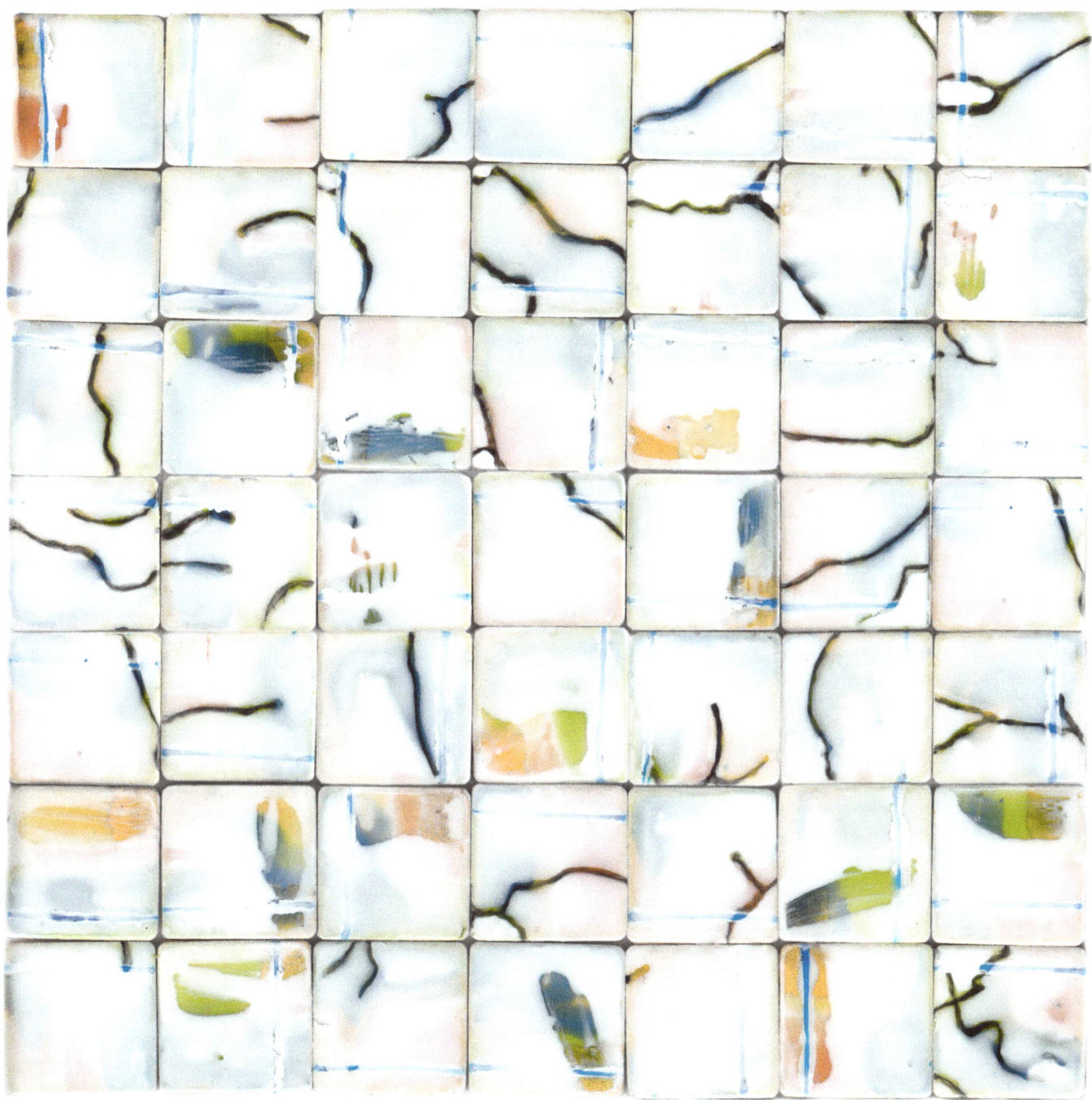

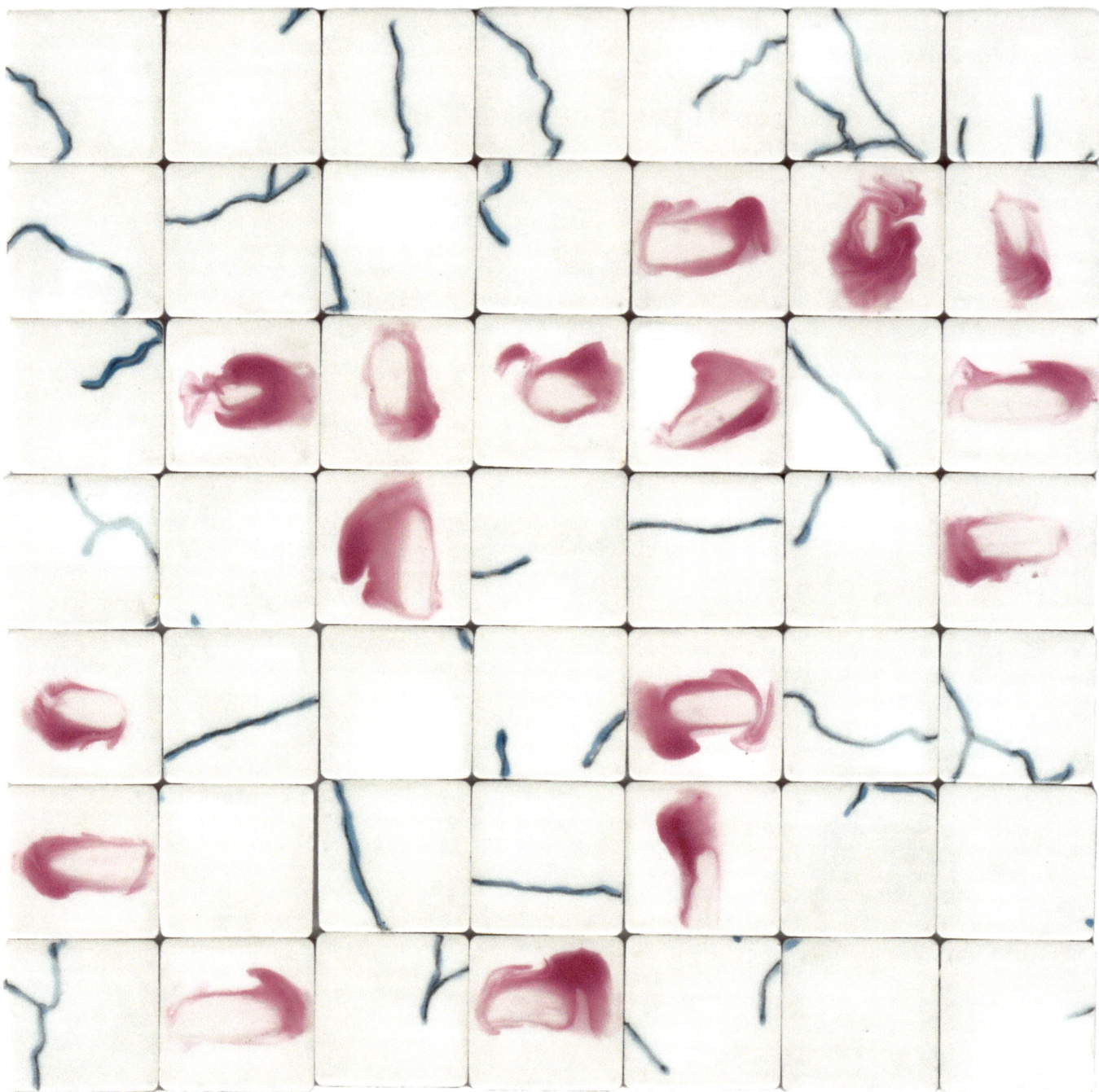

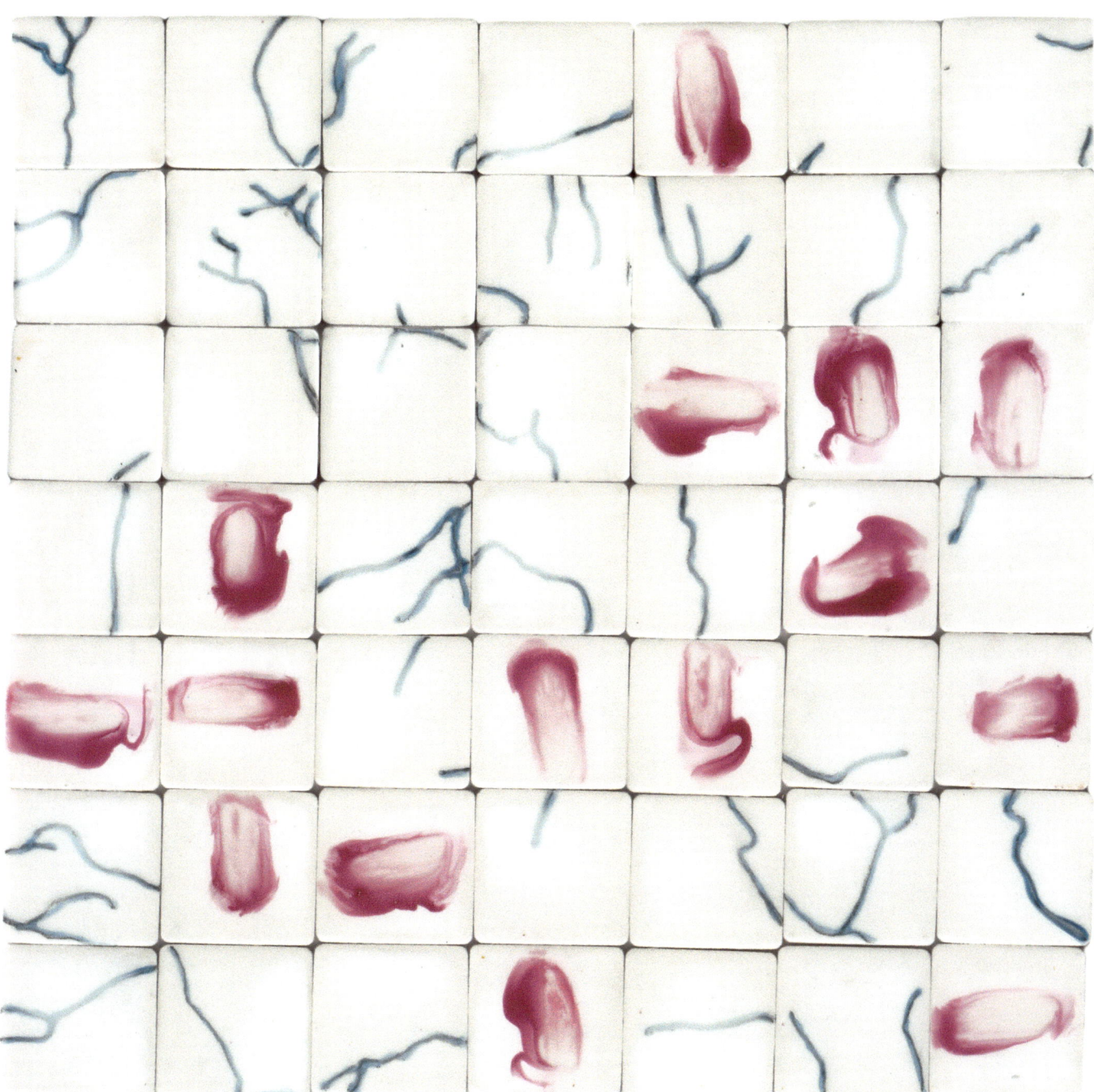

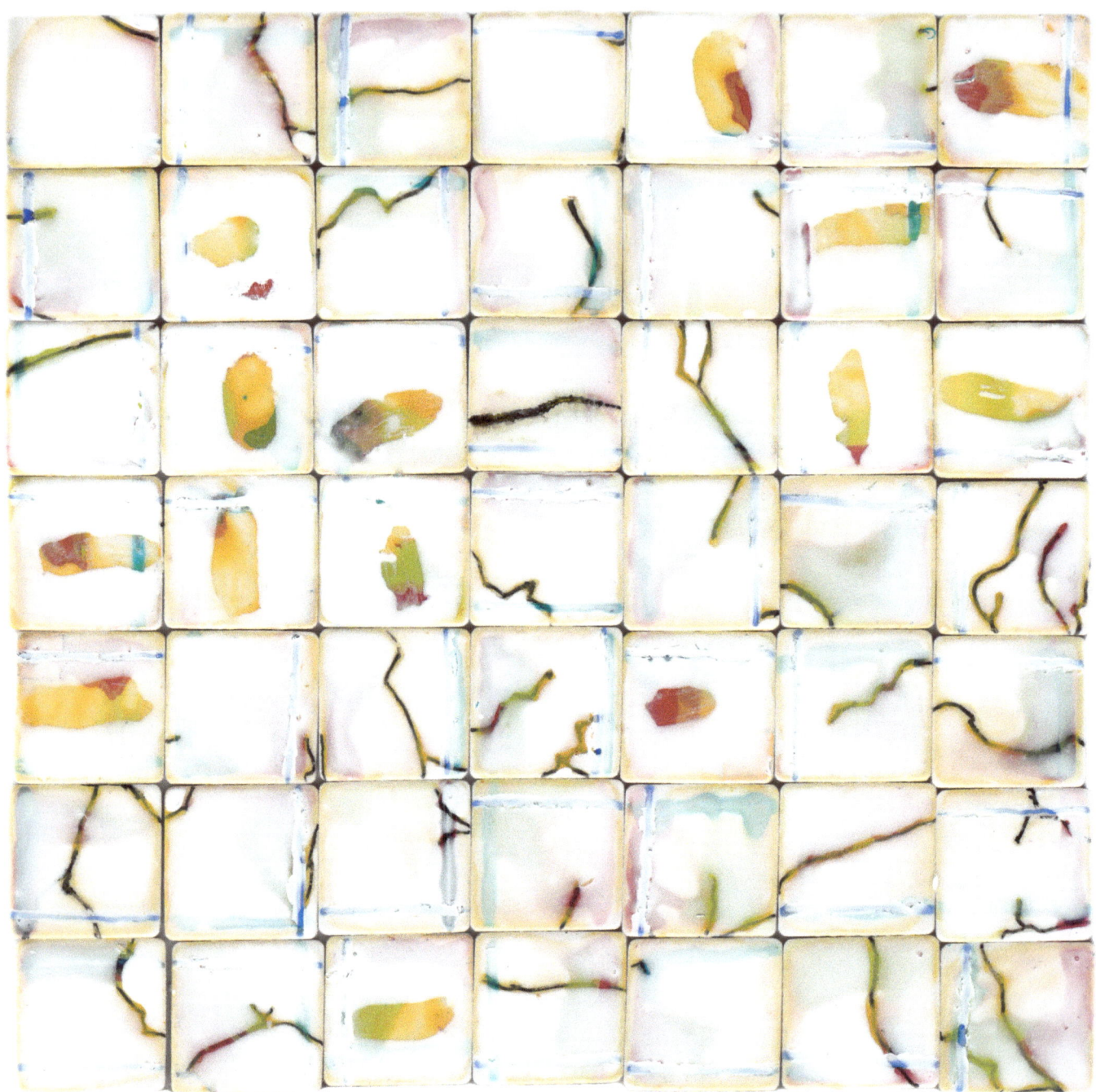

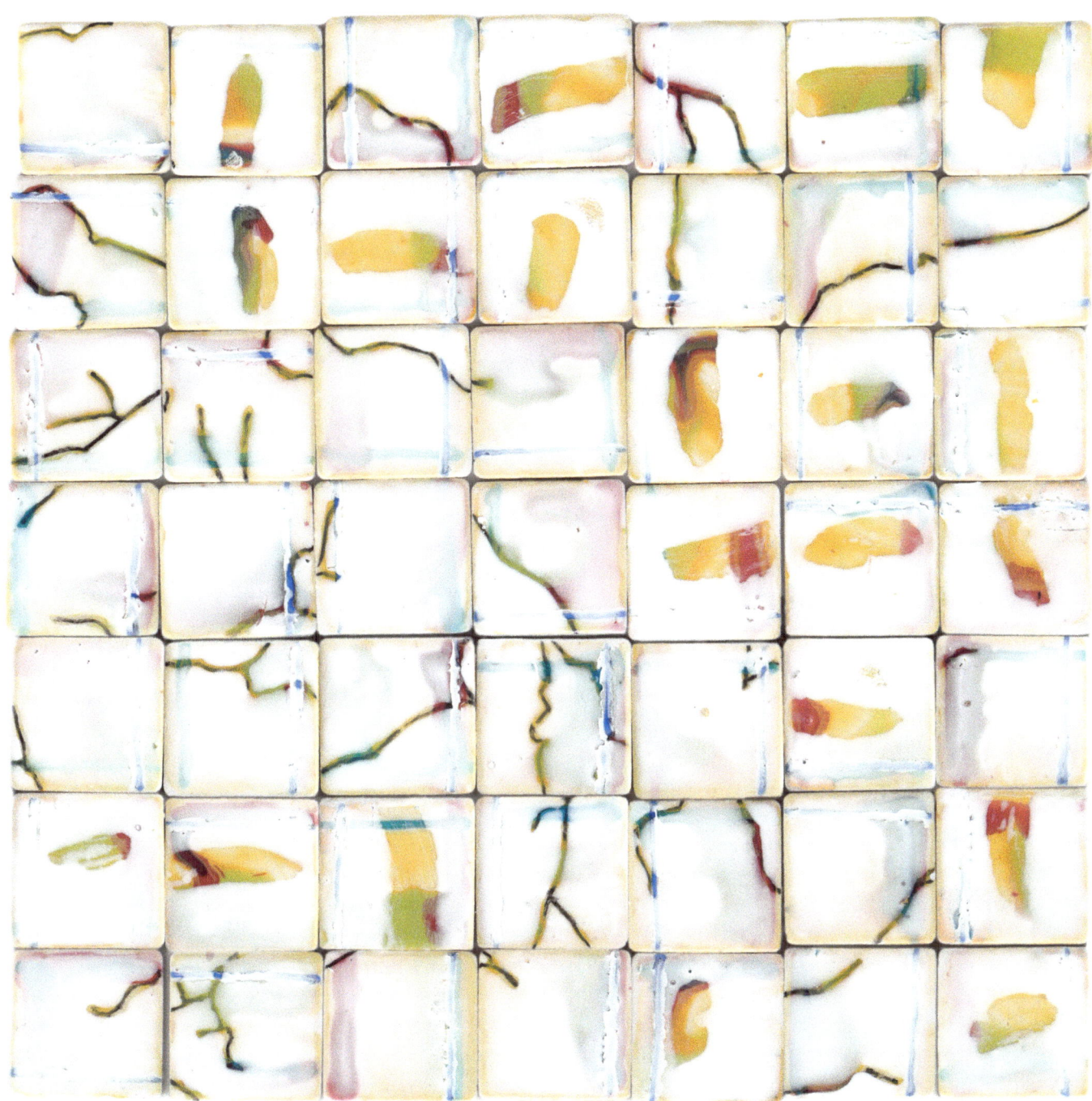

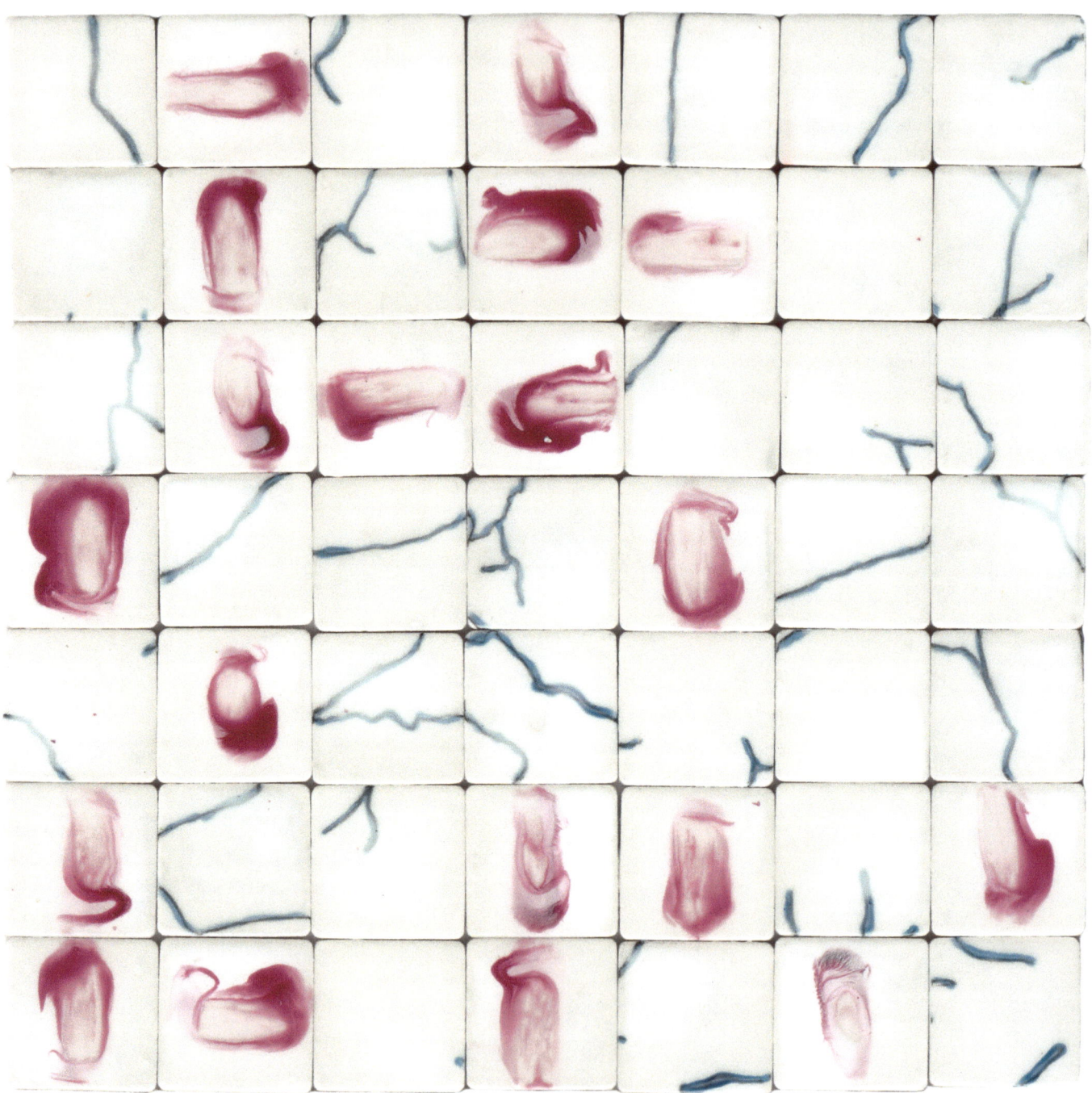

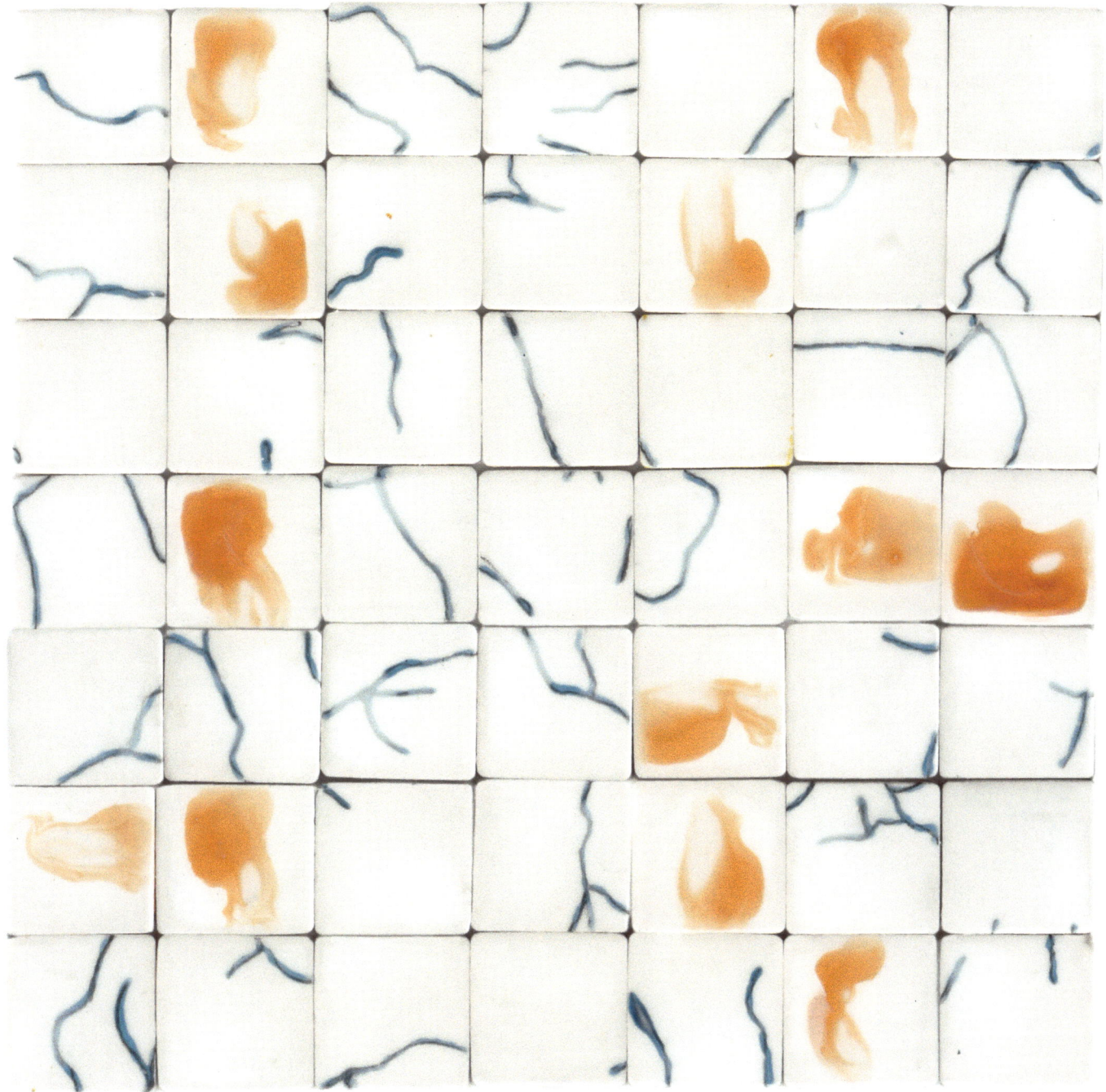

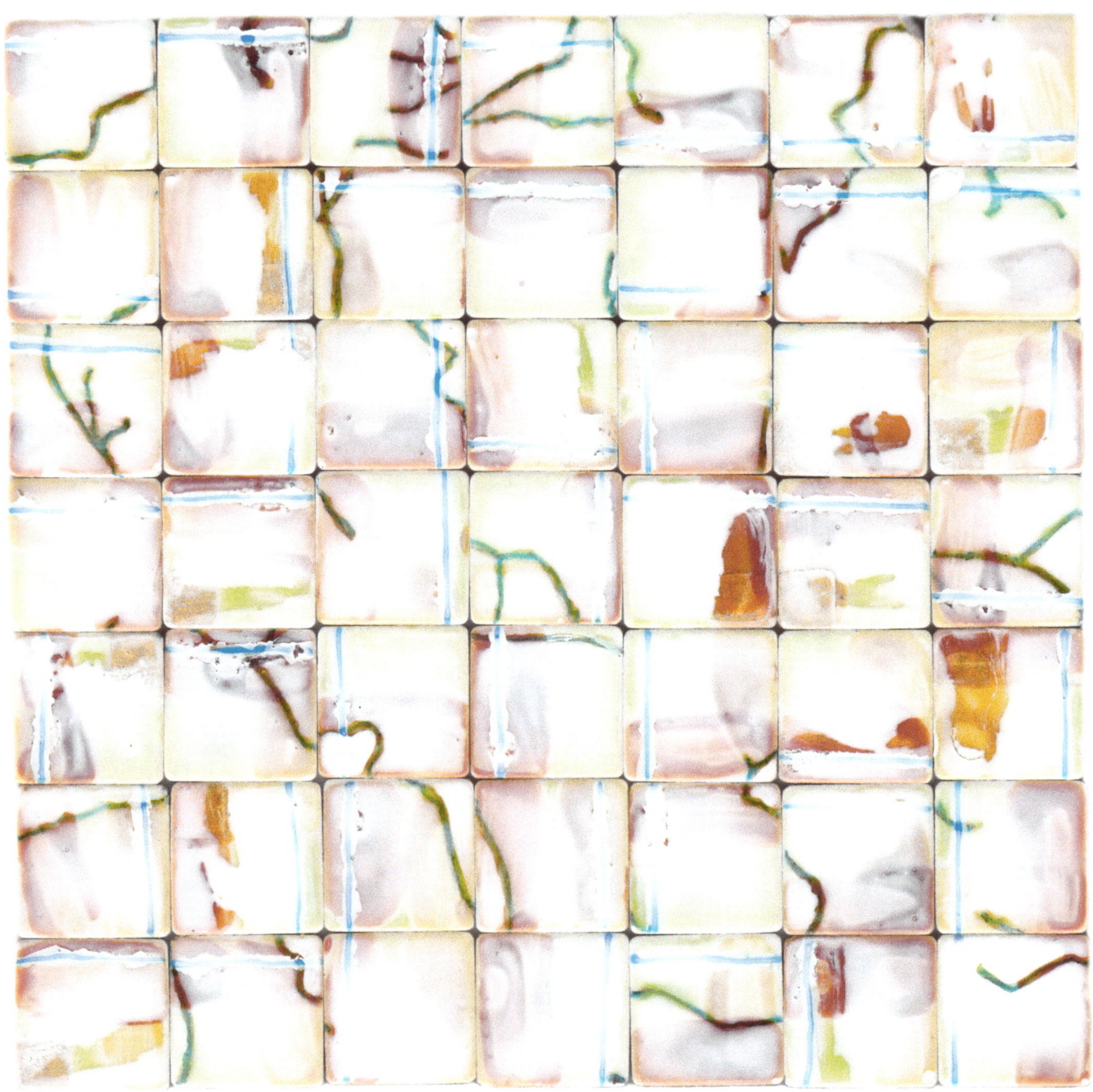

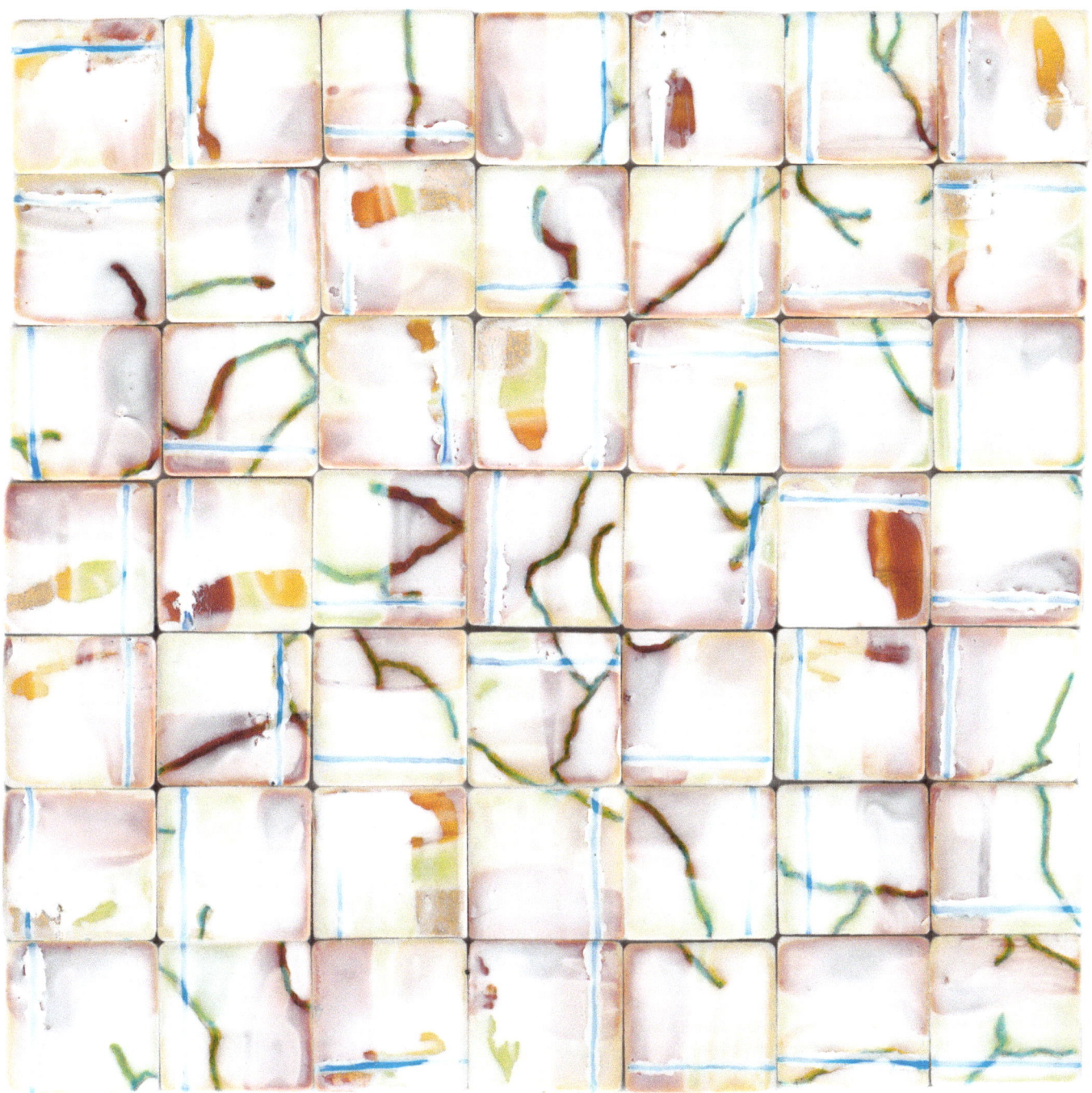

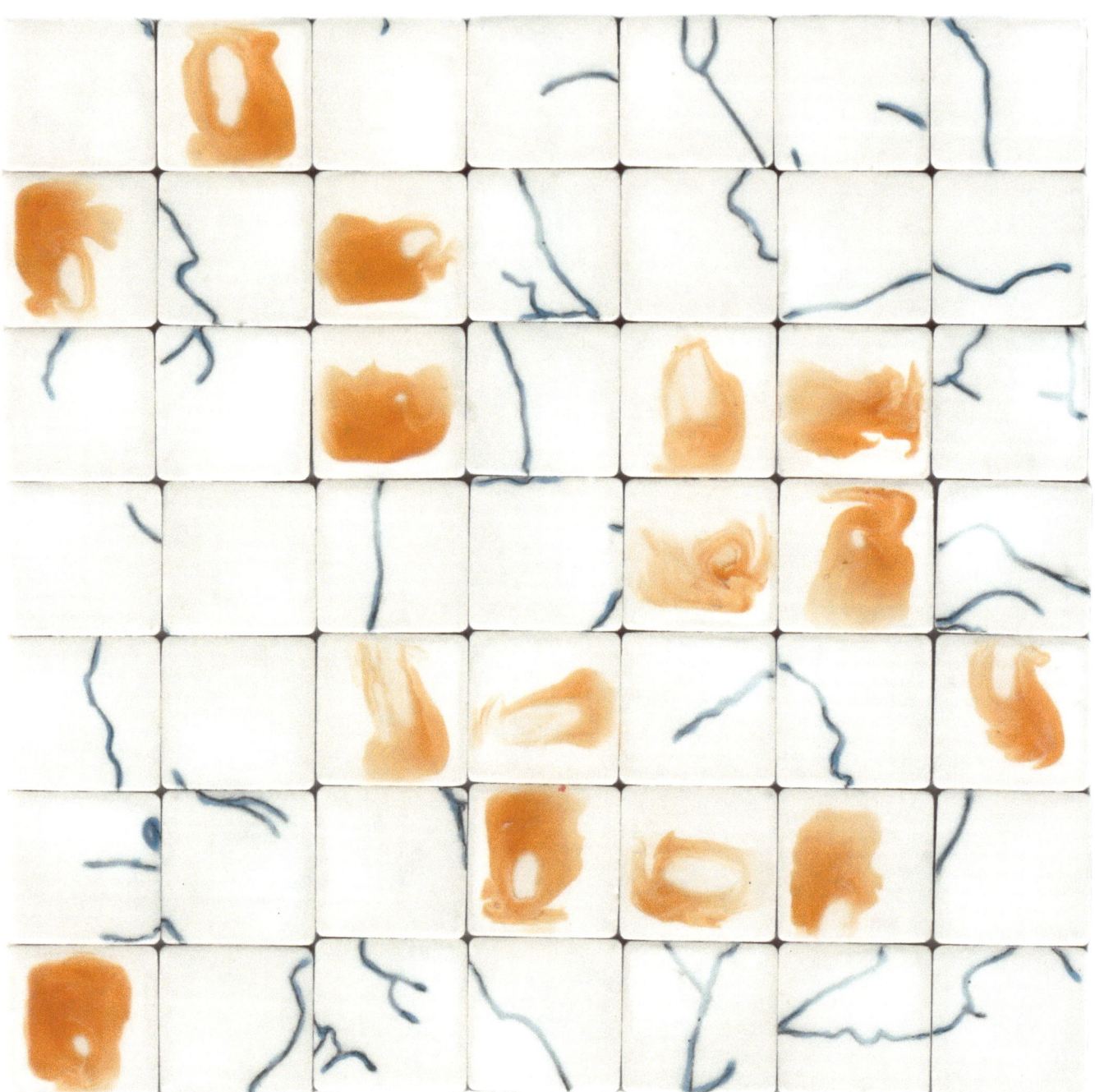

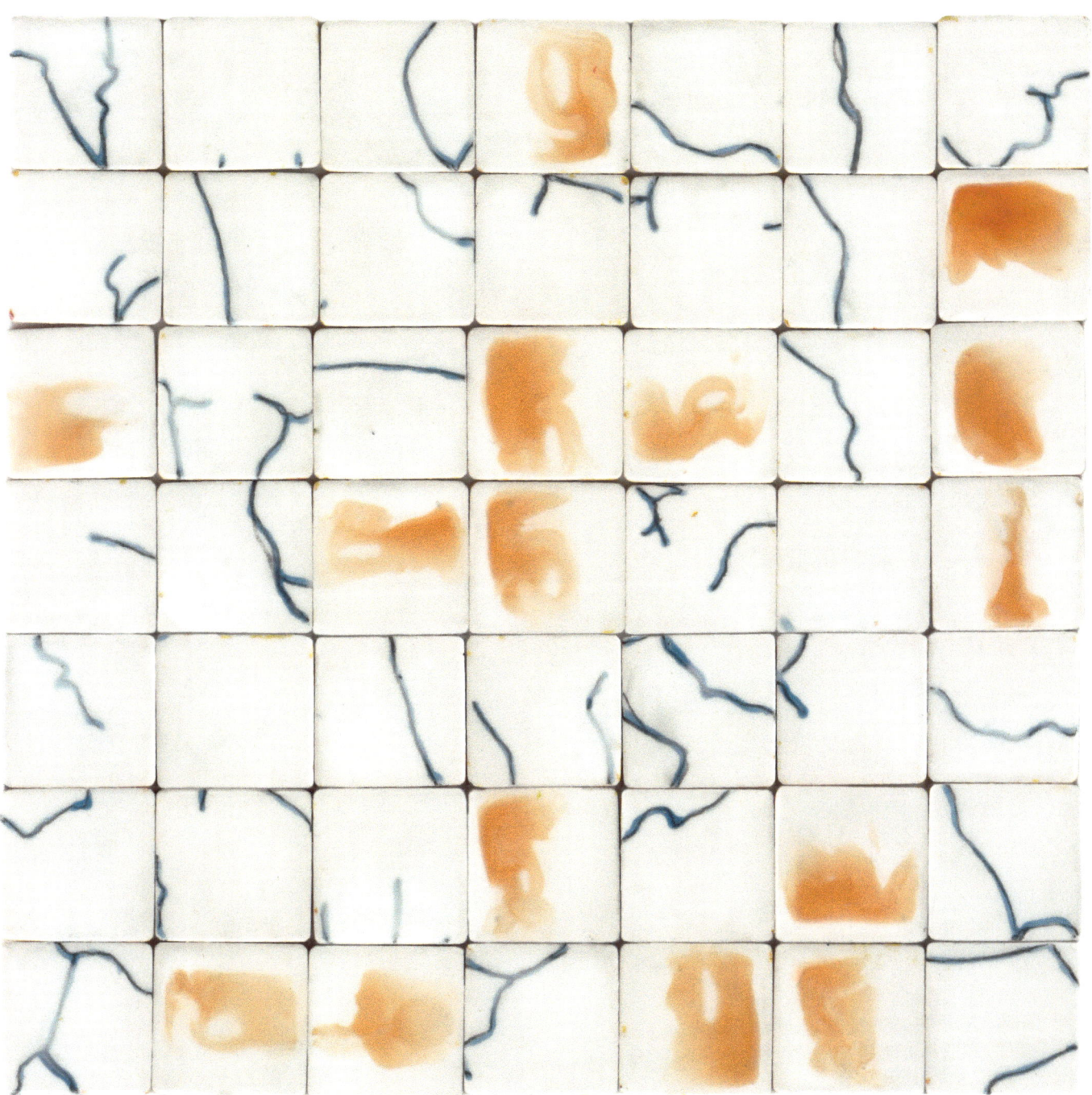

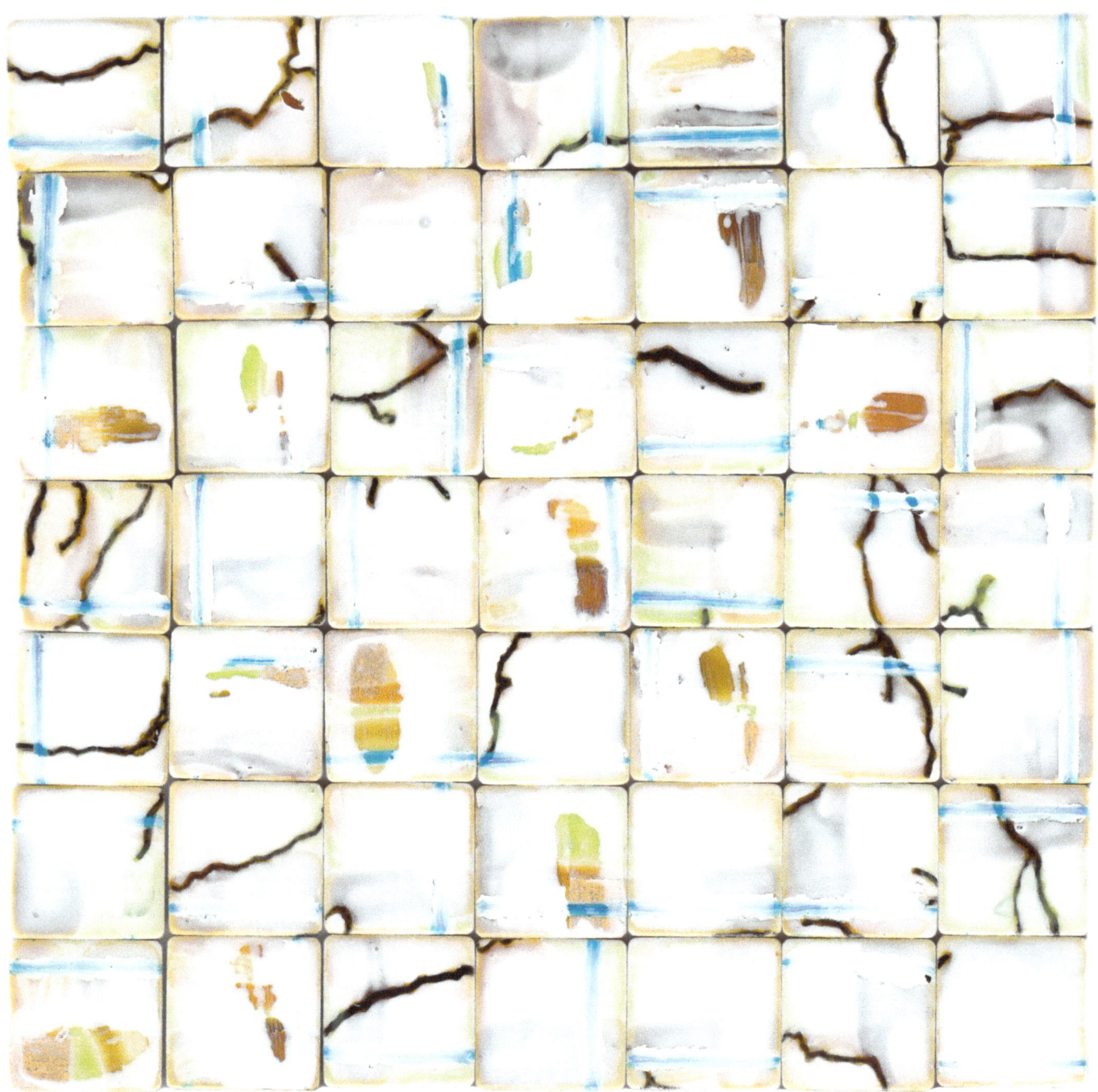

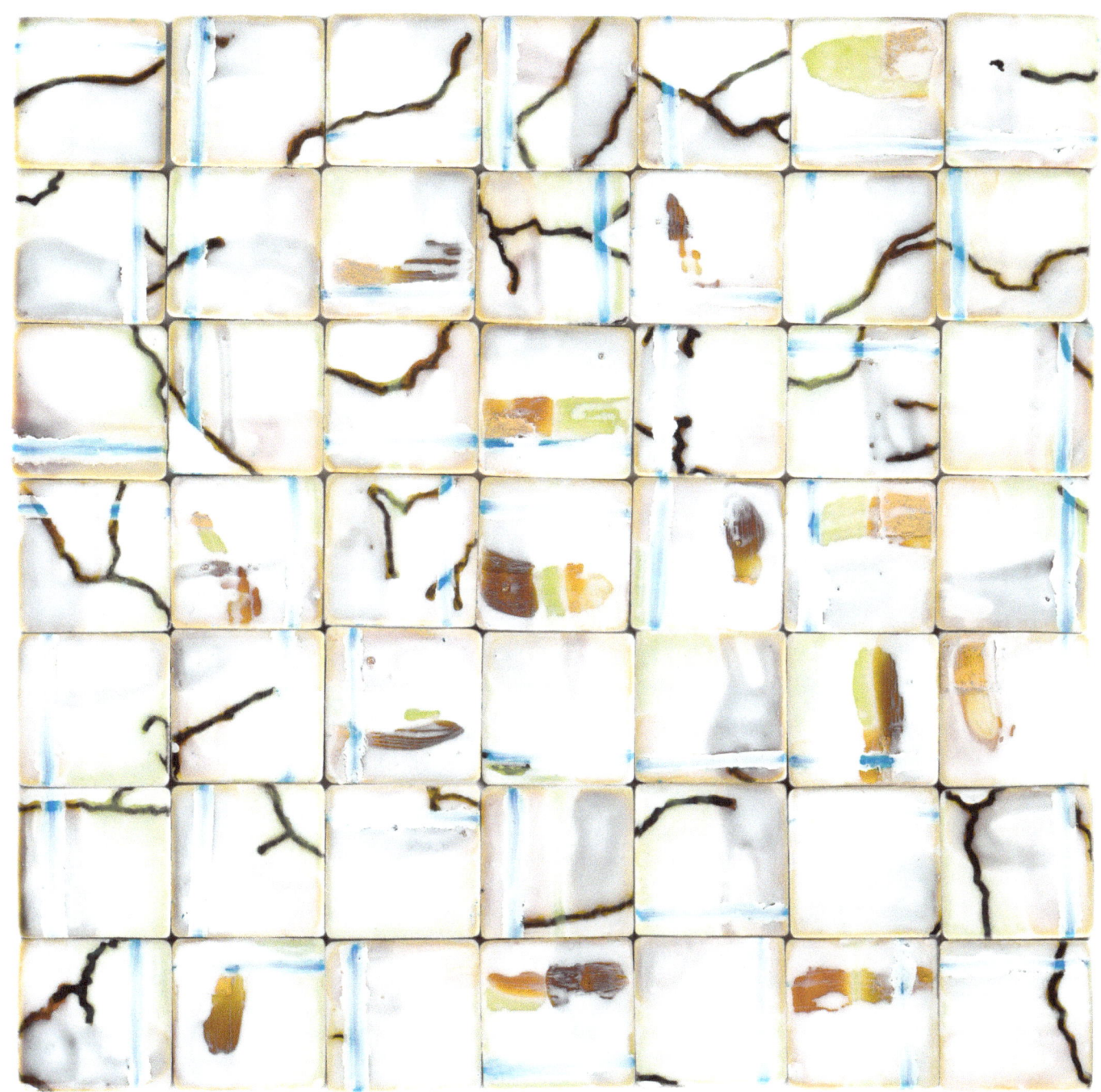

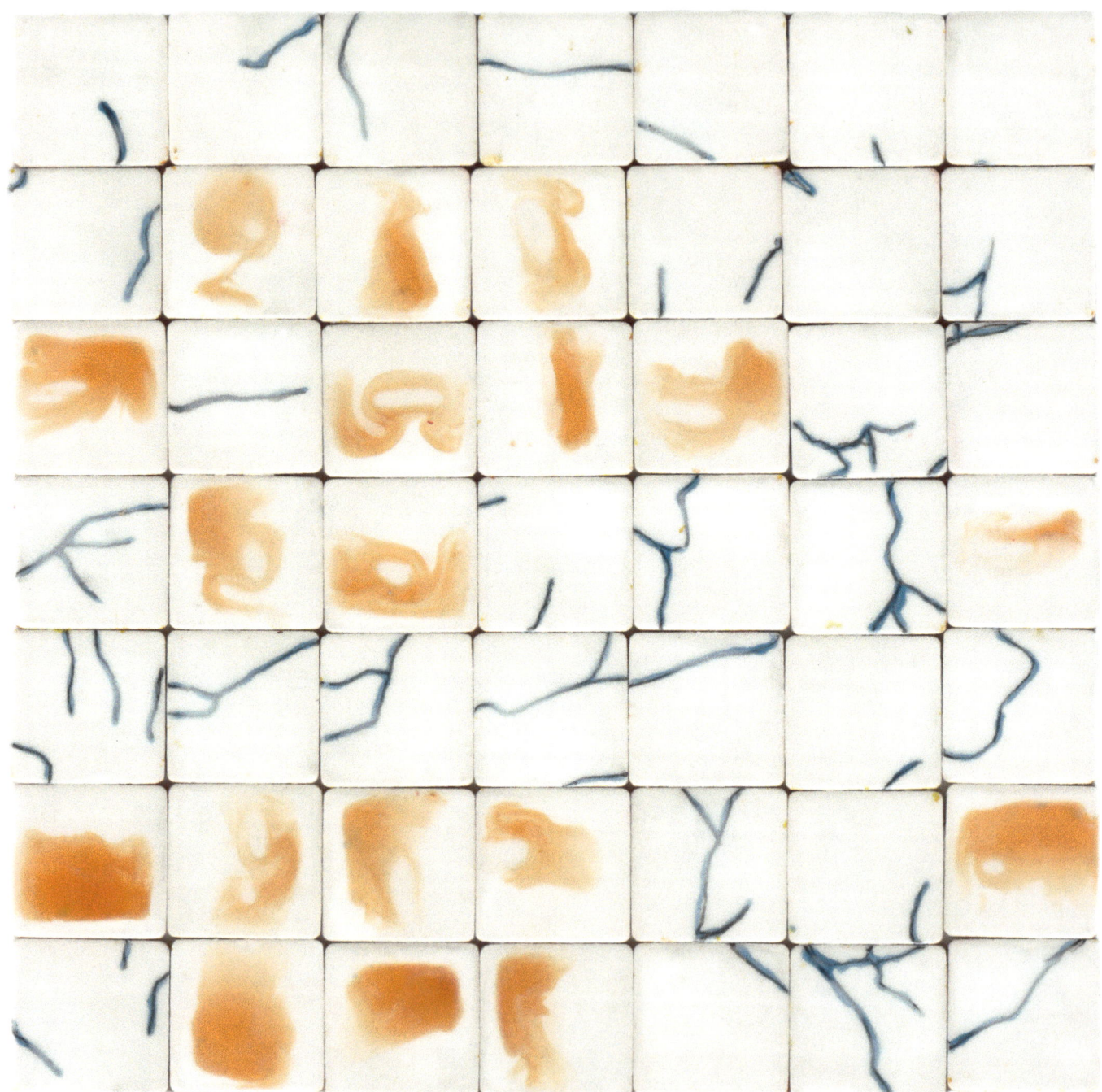

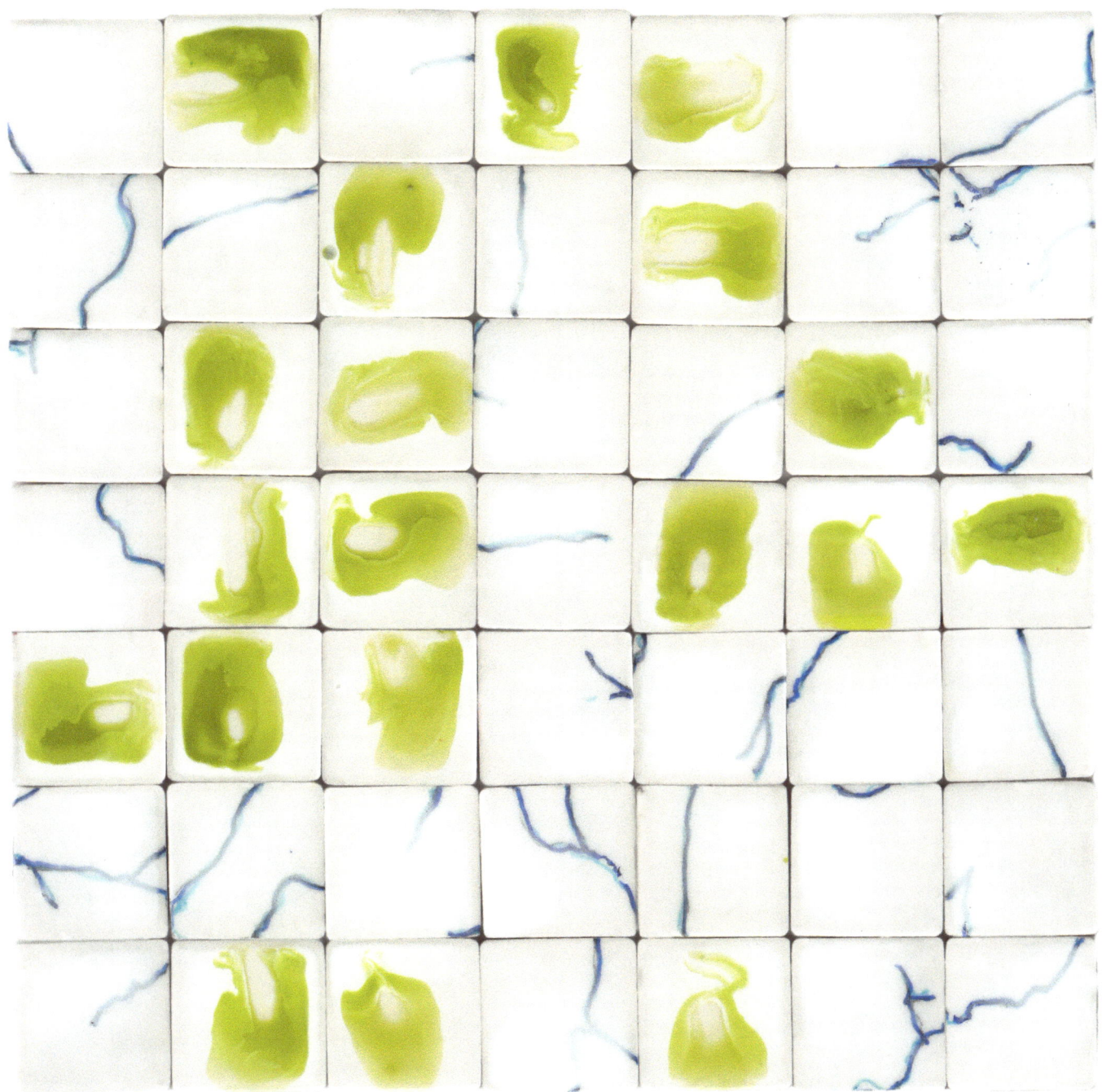

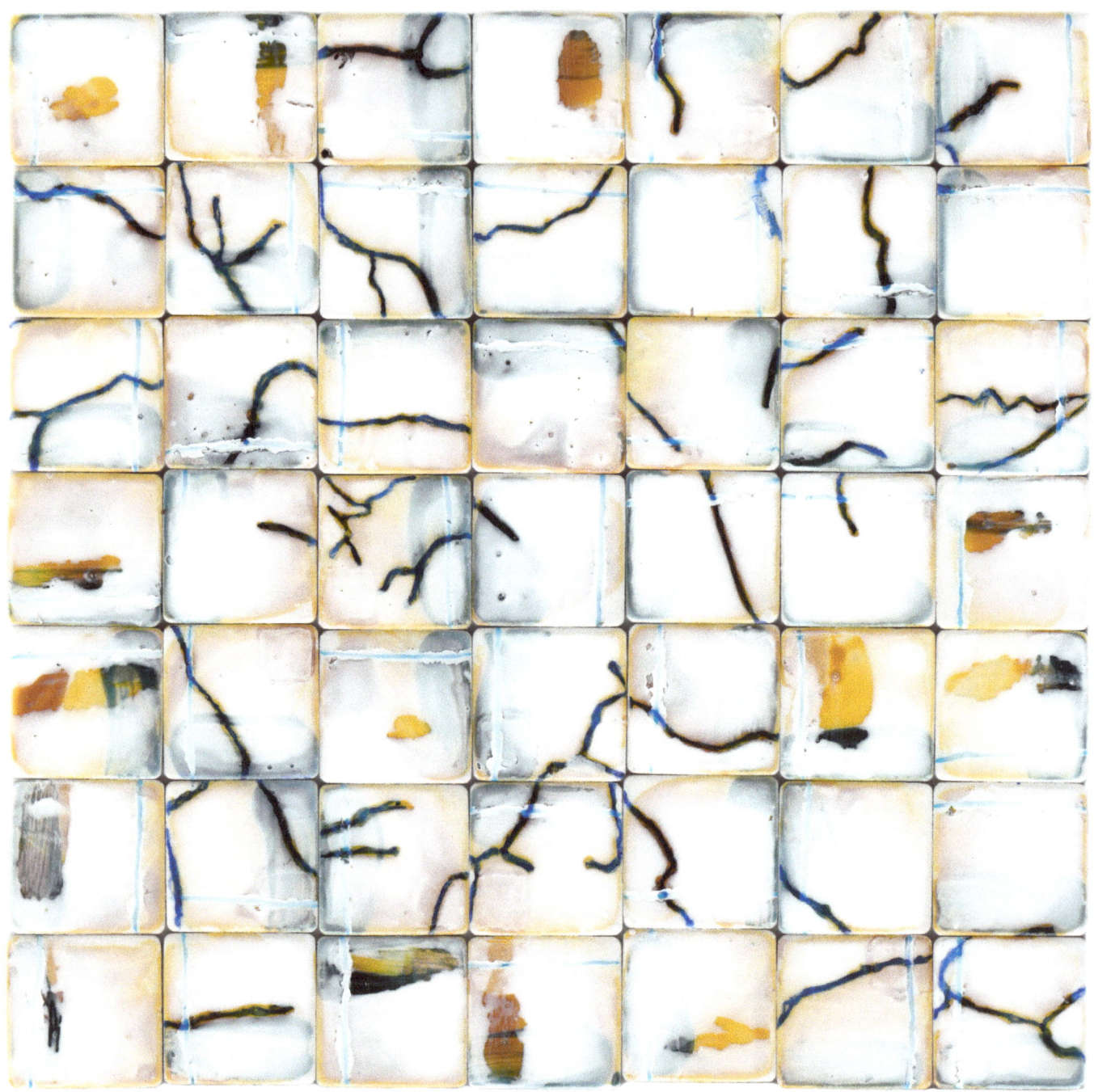

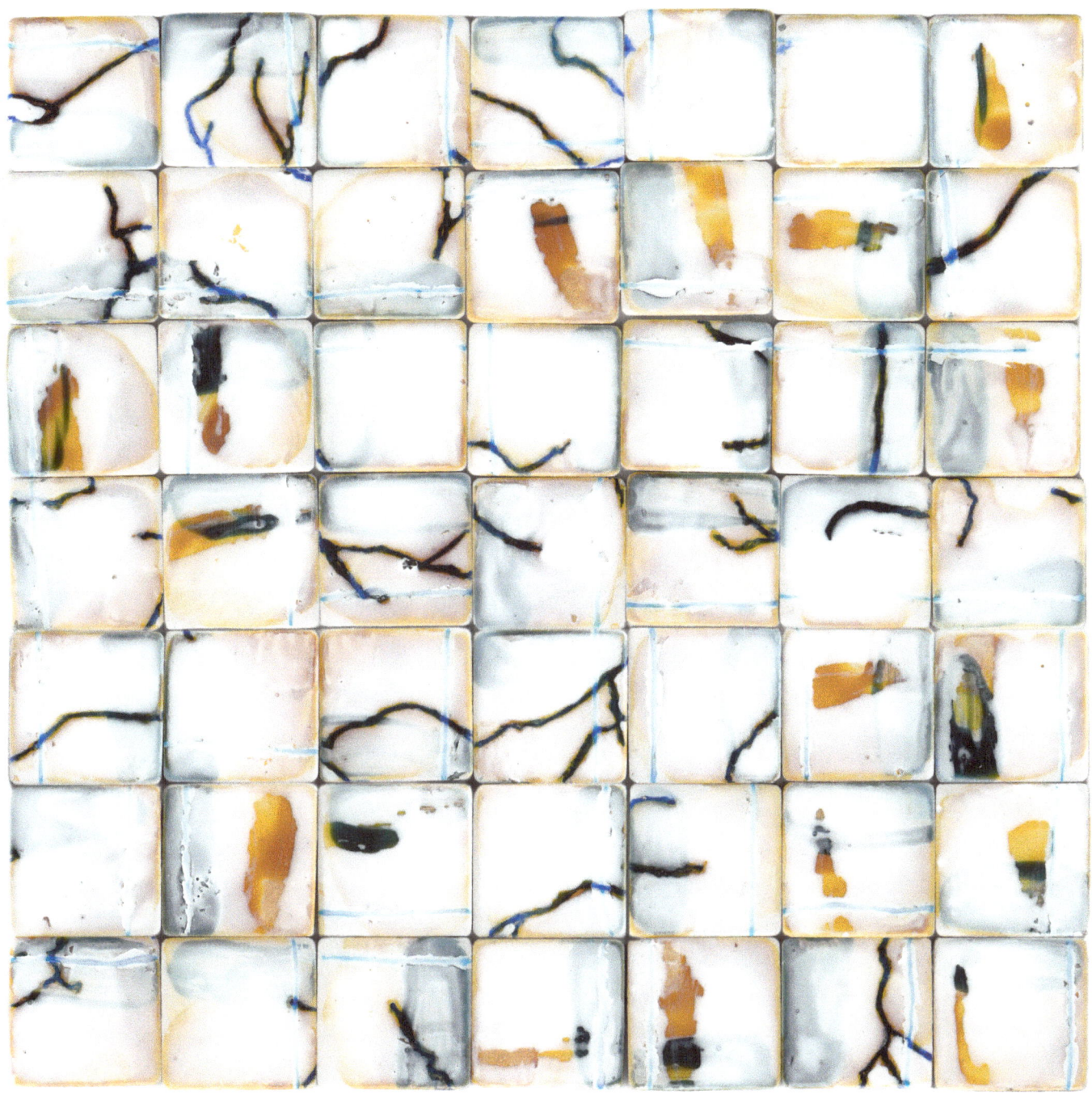

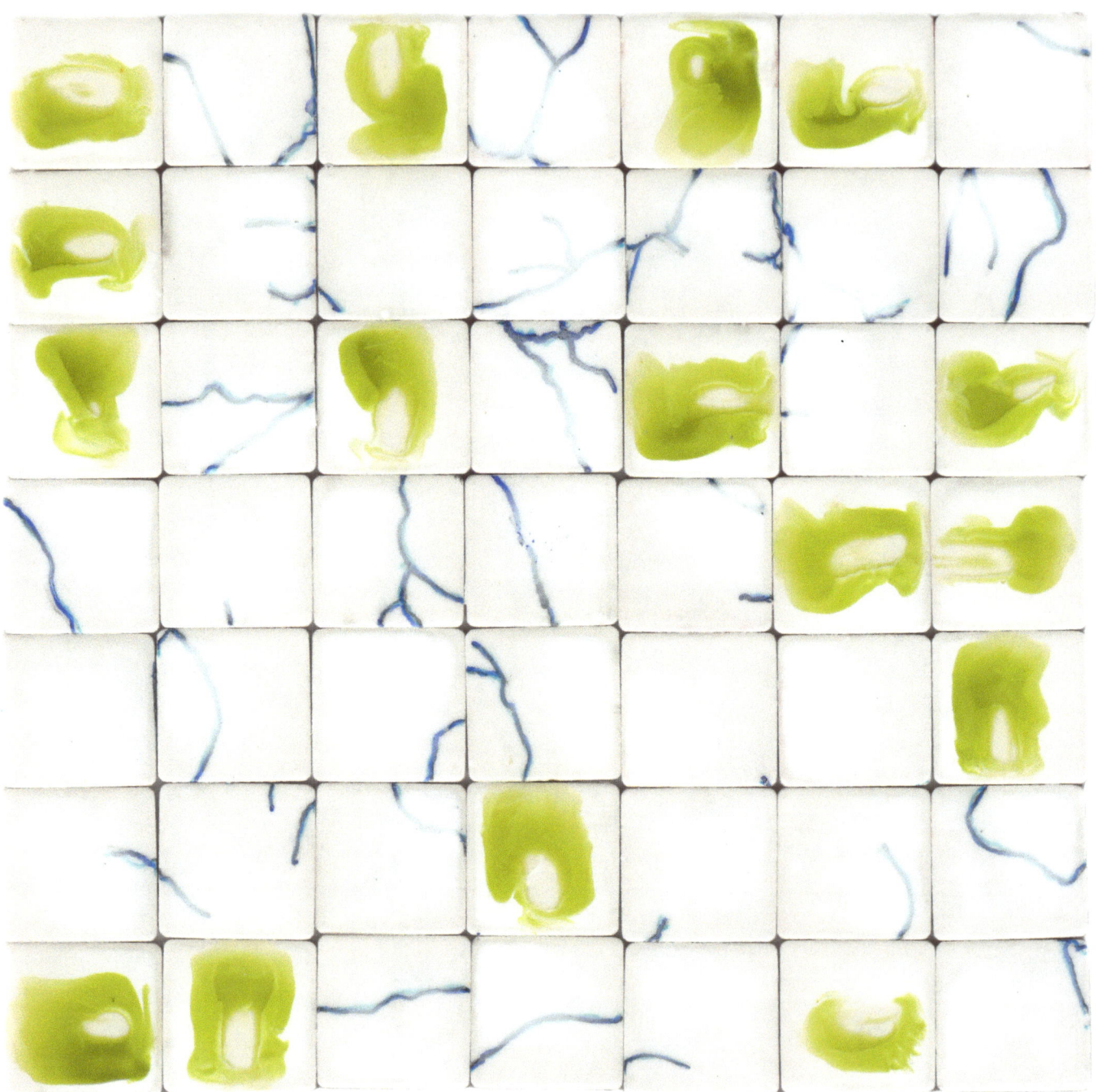

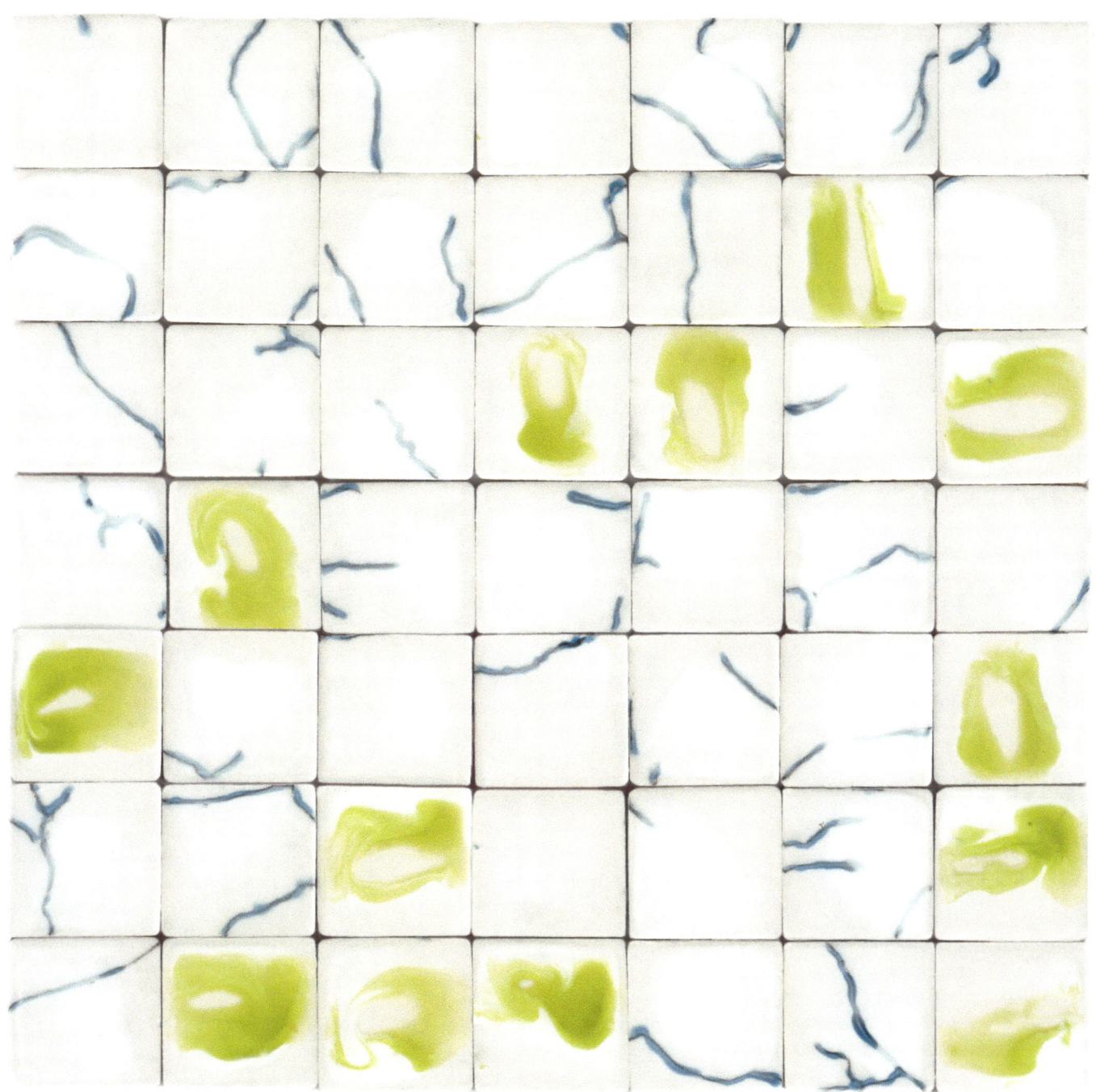

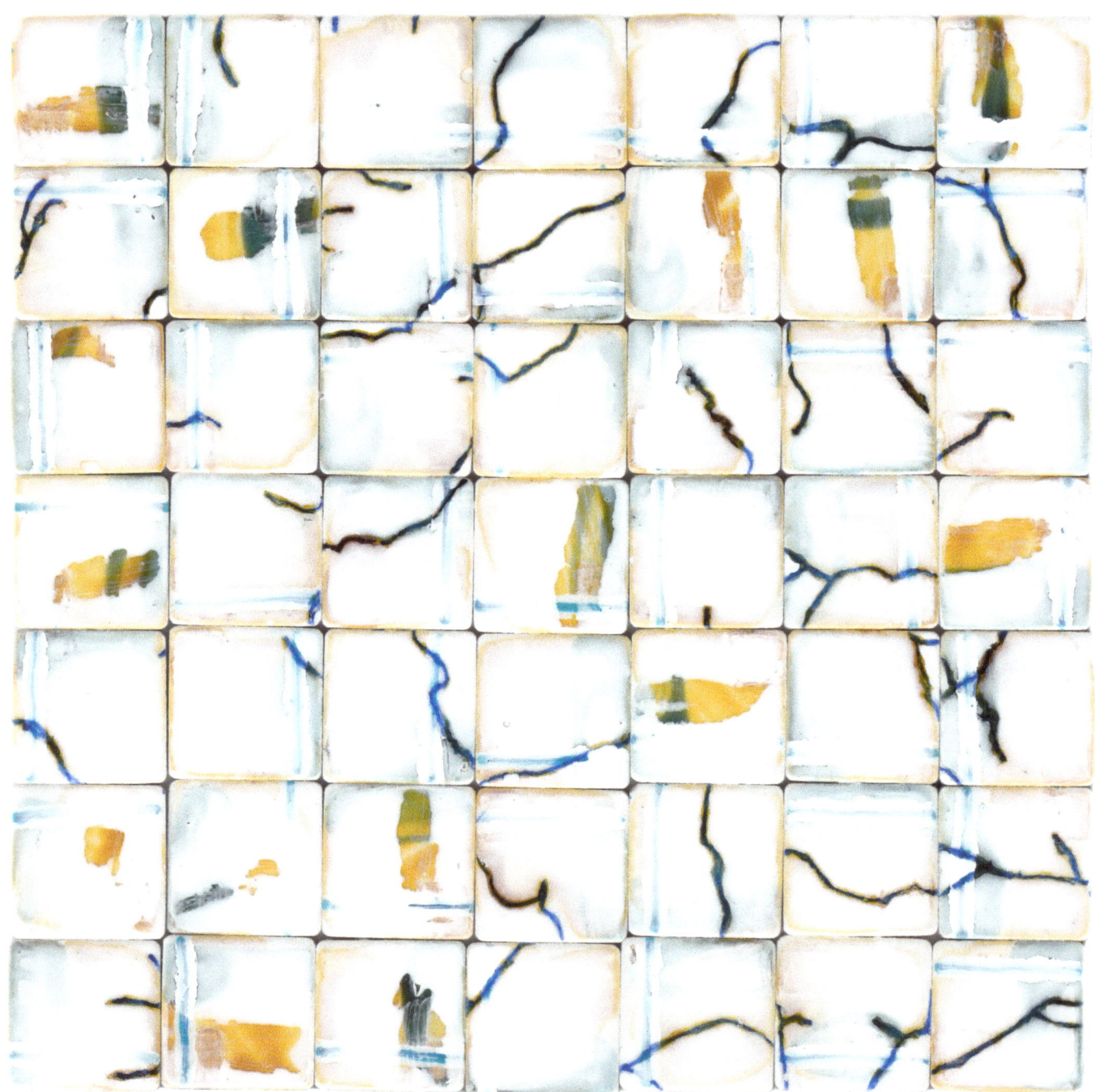

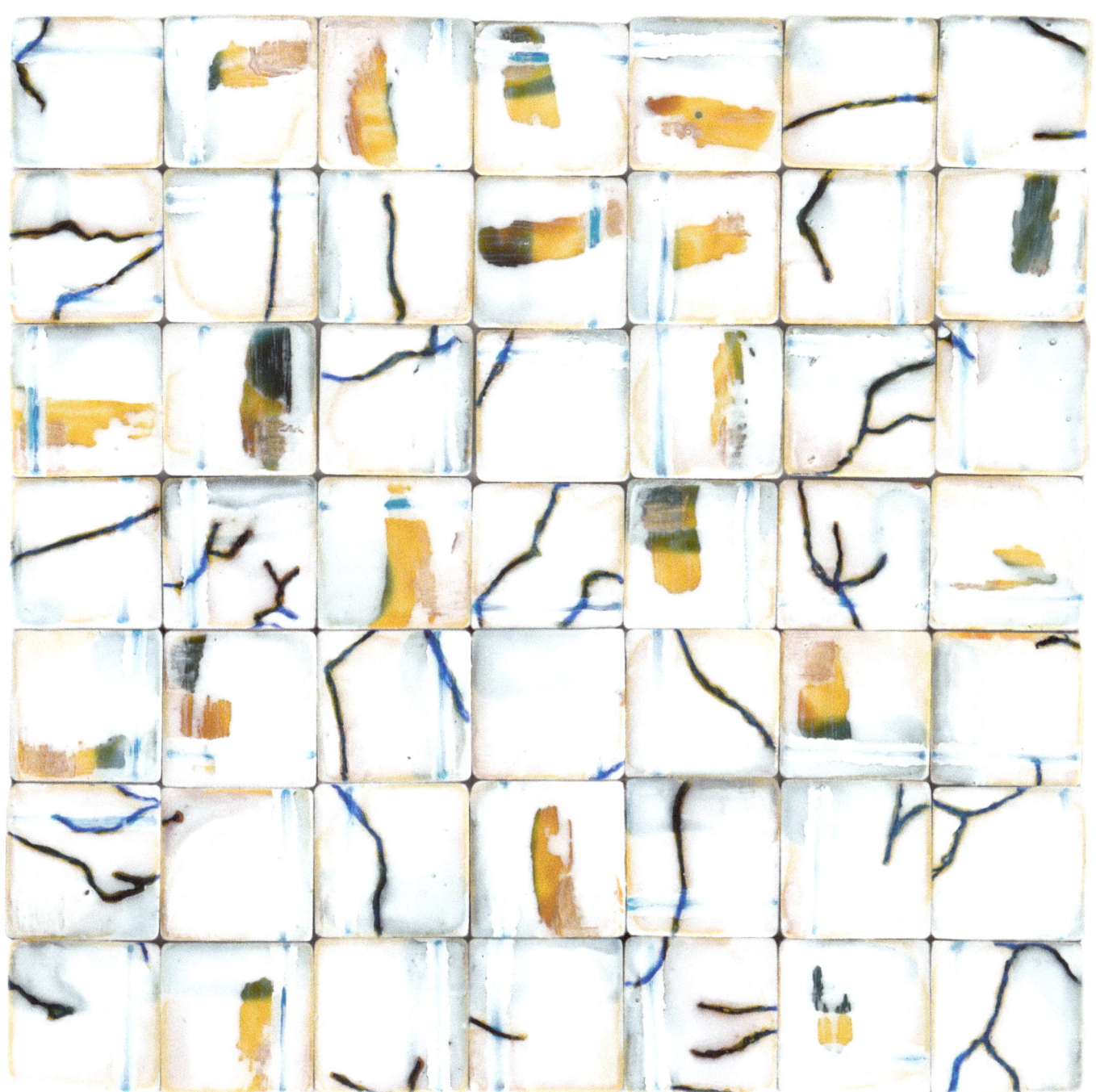

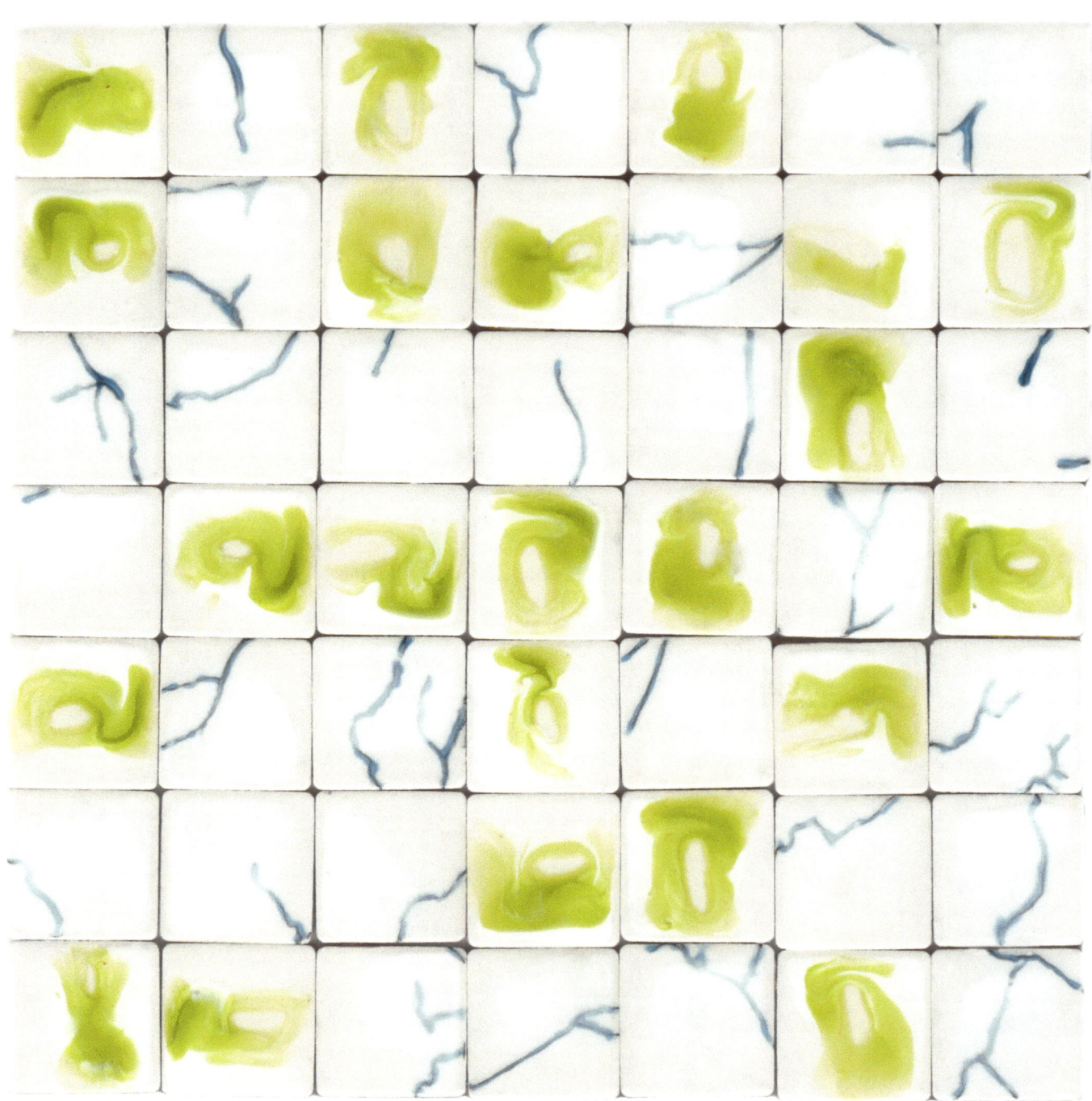

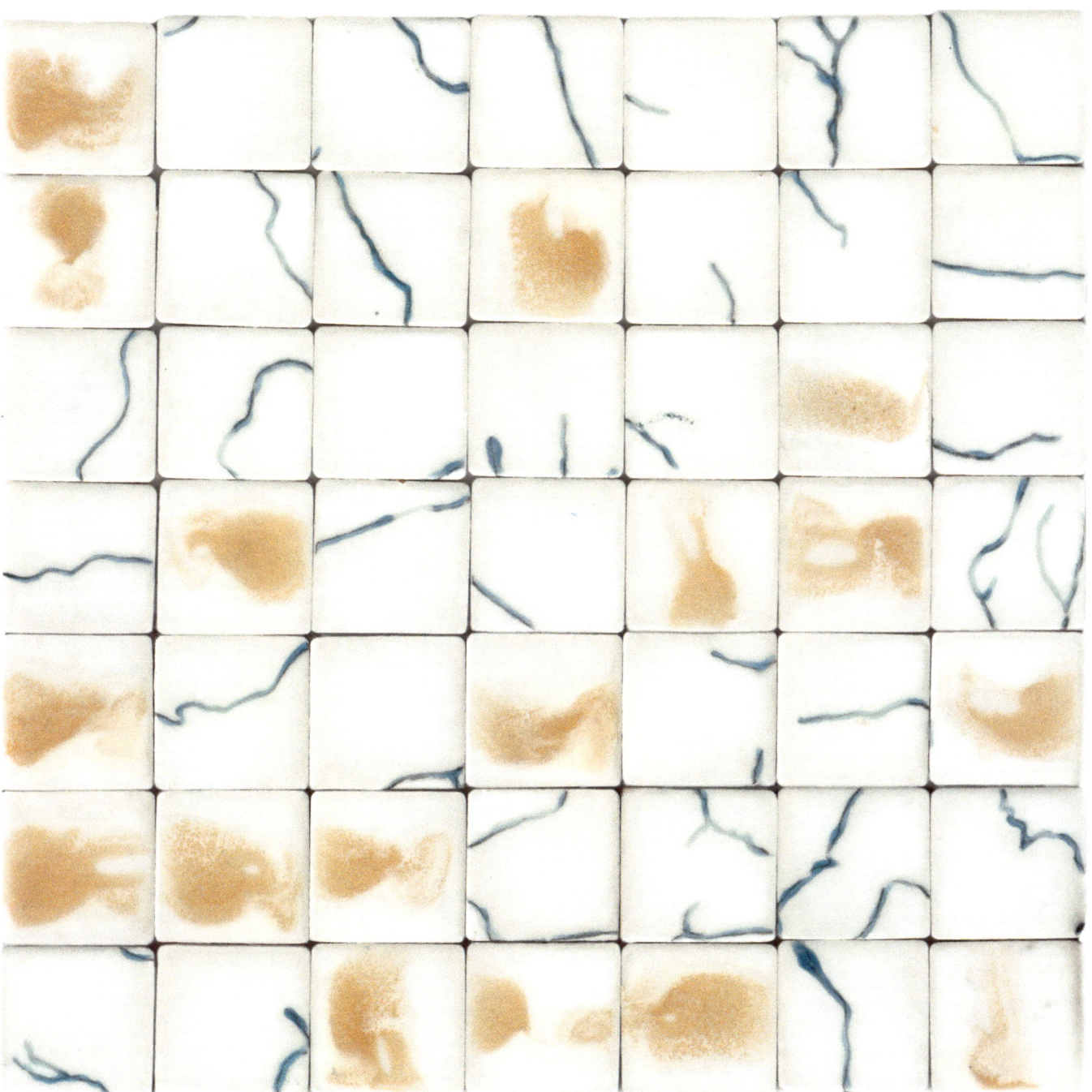

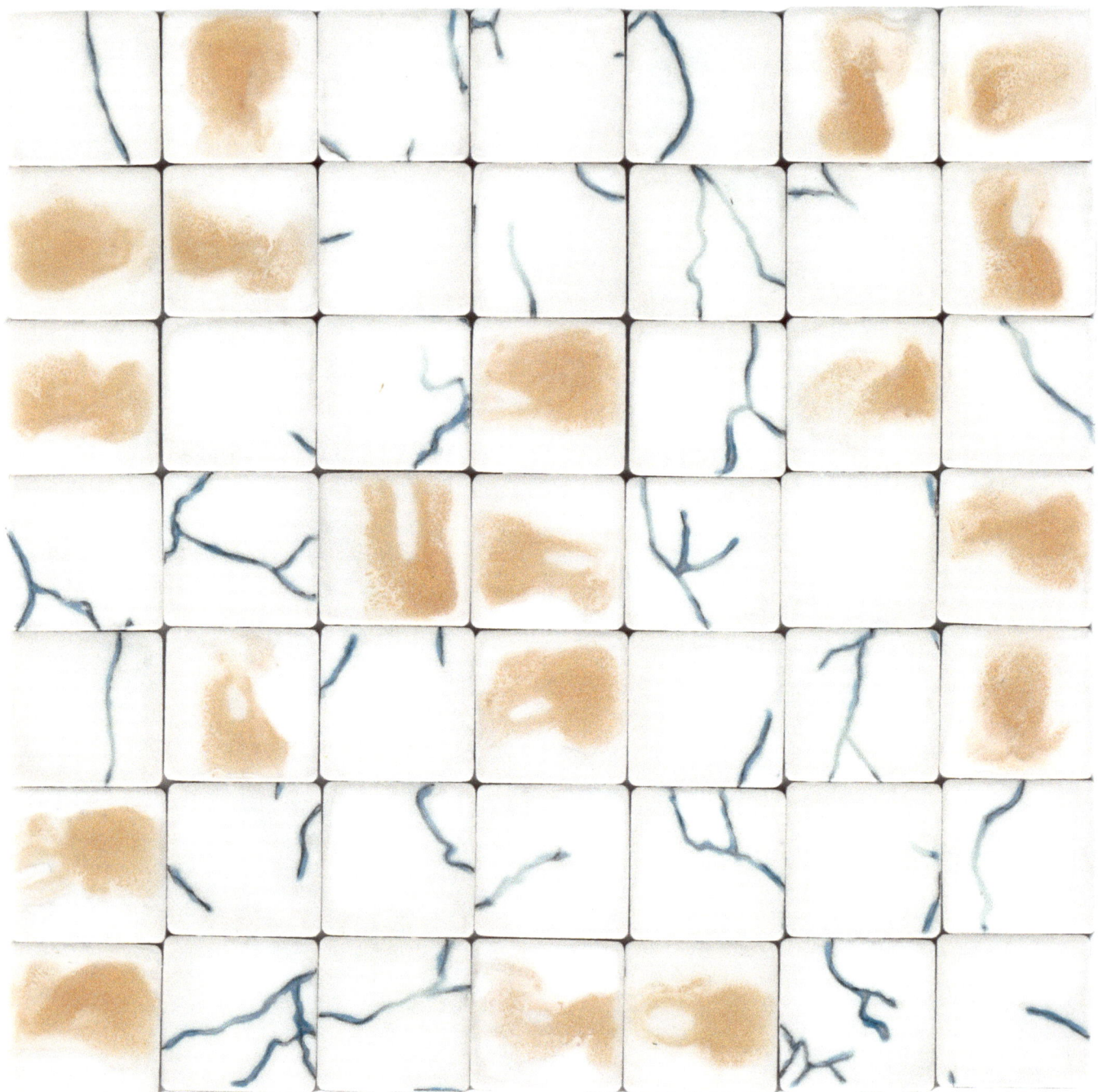

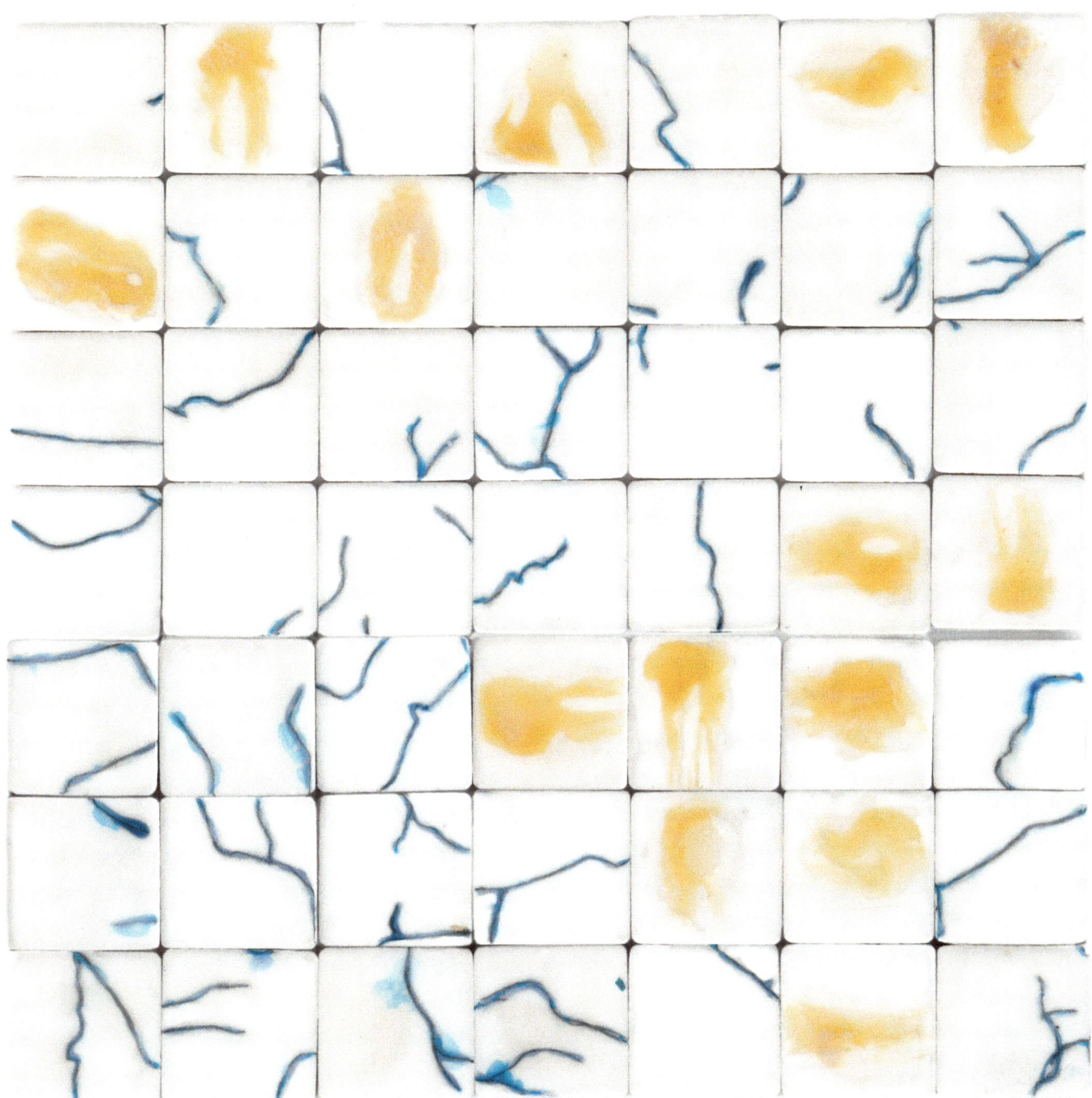

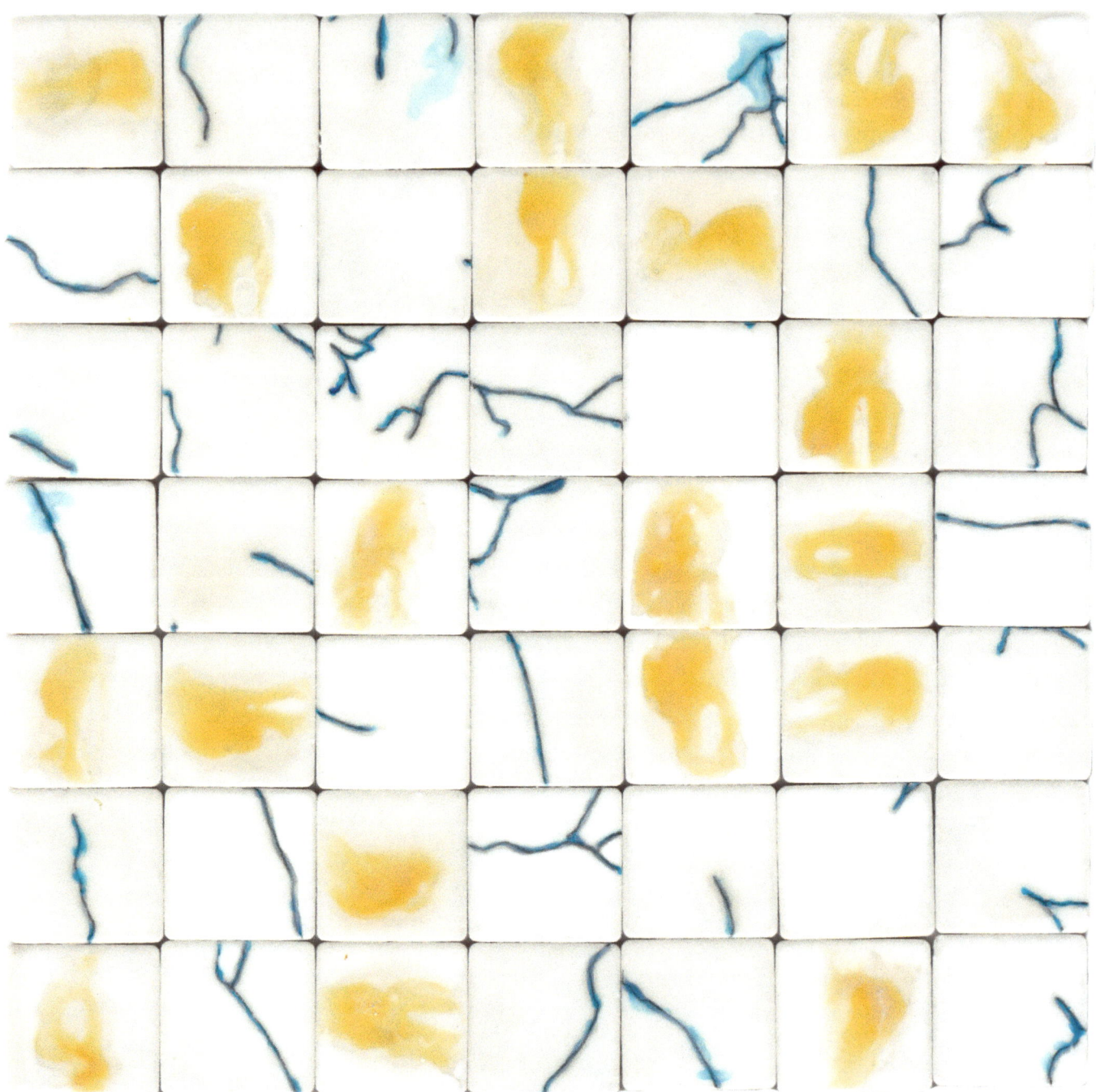

Systems of marking, concealing and revealing. Thinking of Lisbon, Lee Ufan, remembering Athos Bulcão, Maria Lucia Cattani.

Start with a square. A square with four sides, four edges. A square with four corners. One side is marked with colour. The side is chosen at random. Sometimes a square of gold sits in a corner. The corner is chosen at random. The exercise is repeated four times, with varying random numbers from one to four. 100 small squares form one large square. On the large square, traces of London's Lost Rivers. Colours are covered by brush, revealed with finger marks.

100 squares repeated 14 times, sometimes marking edges with colour, sometimes traced lines and finger marks.

Installation at 8 Melior St, Bermondsey, London 2018.
Sets of 100 squares arranged at random in a rows of 2 x 50.

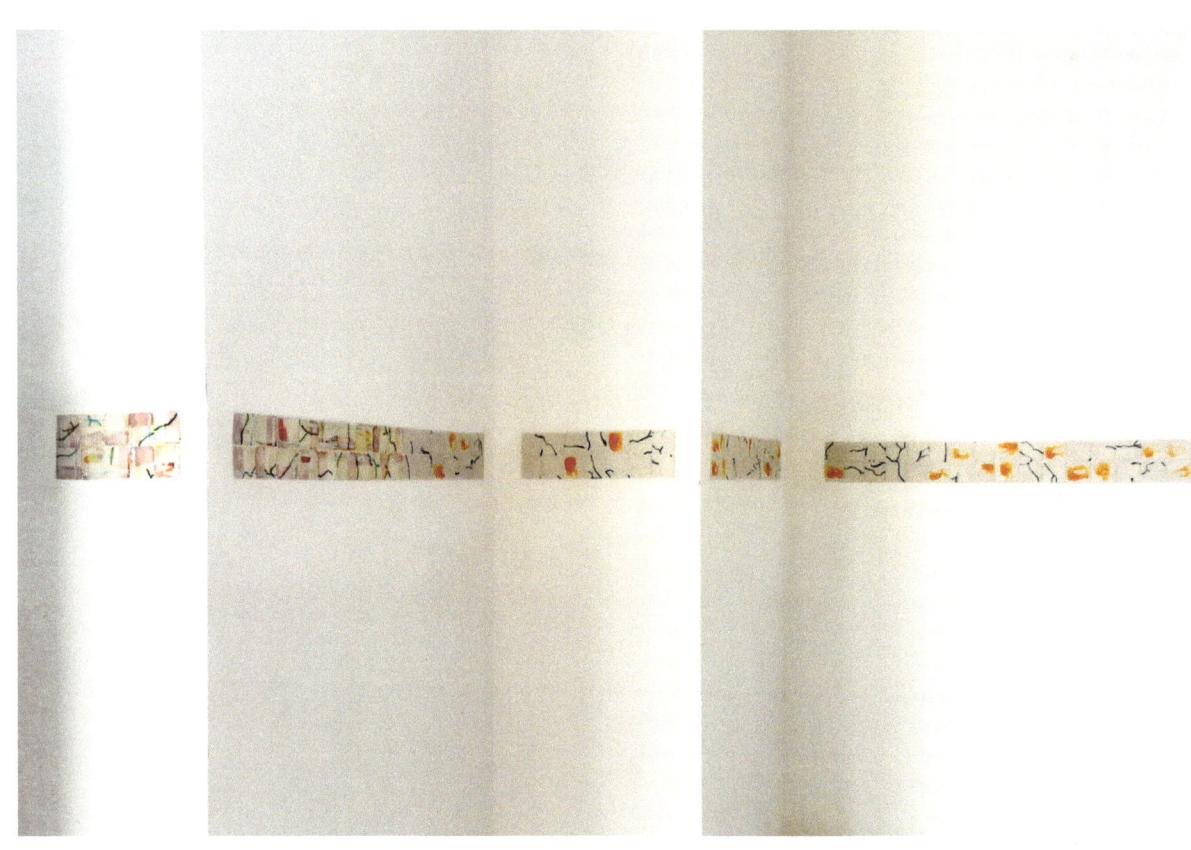

www.nickrands.com